Chelsea House Publishers

Women in the Comics

Maurice Horn

1977
Chelsea House Publishers
New York, London

Picture Research Ass't.: **Richard Marschall**
Creative Director: **Susan Lusk**
Managing Editor: **Laurie Likoff**
Design: **Richard A. Kenerson John Williams Peter Davis**

ISBN: 0-87754-056-X

Horn, Maurice.
Women in the comics.
Includes index.
1. Comic books, strips, etc.—United States—History and criticism. 2. Women in literature. 3. Women in art. I. Title.
PN6725.H6 741.5'973 77-24317
ISBN 0-87754-056-X

CHELSEA HOUSE PUBLISHERS
A Division of Chelsea House Educational Communications, Inc.
Harold Steinberg, Publisher, Chairman Andrew Norman, President
70 West 40 Street, New York 10018

Acknowledgments

Many people have helped with documentation, suggestions and advice during the planning and realization of this book. It is a pleasure to express my sincere appreciation to: Bill Blackbeard, Jerry Iger, Burne Hogarth, Dorothy Herscher, Jerry Muller, John Knight, Susan Lusk and Maryvonne Fortier; a special note of thanks to Richard Marschall for his invaluable assistance in researching the illustrations for this book.

Acknowledgment is also extended to King Features Syndicate, the Chicago Tribune-New York News Syndicate, NEA Service, Marvel Comics Group, DC Comics Inc, ERB, Inc., United Feature Syndicate, McNaught Syndicate, Universal Press Syndicate, Editions du Lombard, Le Terrain Vague, Milano Libri, and the National Cartoonists Society.

Finally I wish to thank my publisher, Harold Steinberg, whose well-documented interest in the subject provided the original impetus for this book.

Also by the Author

A History of the Comic Strip (with Pierre Couperie), 1968
75 Years of the Comics, 1971
The World Encyclopedia of Comics (ed.), 1976
Comics of the American West, 1977

In Preparation:

The World Encyclopedia of Cartoons

Contents

INTRODUCTION

I have carried the idea of this book for quite some time; yet it is through an irony of history that it should come out at this particular point in time. The subject stands at the confluence of two major cultural currents of the 1970's: the growing recognition of the comics as a legitimate and original art form, and the increased acceptance of the feminine condition as an unresolved and volatile problem in the broader context of Western culture.

It would be, therefore, quite understandable on the part of some observers to expect from this volume more than was originally intended. This is a study of the image of woman as perceived through the comics, not an exhaustive inquiry into the medium's treatment of women and its effect on the culture at large (although these aspects are by necessity touched upon). The study focuses mainly on American comics (newspaper strips and comic books), as the American production has been both the most numerous over the years and the most archetypal (as evidenced by its worldwide acceptance). Although the grouping of chapters in this volume is by decade—in order to show the change in attitudes and perception from one ten-year period to the next—I have tried not to take a literal view of chronology, but to put more emphasis on similarities of theme or outlook between features originated within the same decade.

There is a generous amount of illustrations, as there should be in a work of this nature, since the graphic *appearance* of women in the comics is at least as important as their outlook and character. The leading women characters —as well as some of their more obscure sisters—are presented in the framework of each decade in which they appeared and flourished, with concise accompanying information as to the origins, background, style and plot line of the strips that featured them. Again formal chronology is not strictly adhered to in the examples that were selected. When the atmosphere, way of dress, style of a particular decade were important to the understanding of a given strip, the example would be taken from that period. On the other hand, when the spirit, the flavor, the *Zeitgeist* of a particular strip or character were carried over the years (and this is the case of the most enduring features) the example might be taken from a later decade. The criterion here was exemplarity—the essence of the character as given regardless of time.

The delicate balance that exists between male and female characters in the comics has not escaped the critical scrutiny of sociologists, psychologists and mass communication experts. One such study (fittingly titled "Male and Female Relations in the American Comic Strip"), conducted by Gerhart Saenger, appeared in 1955. Saenger's analysis was based on all comic strips appearing in the (then) nine leading New York City newspapers during October, 1950. Some of the findings are interesting (if hardly conclusive, based as they are on such a narrow sample): the most revealing one documents the reversal of life roles between male and female before and after marriage.

Saenger found that while the male was traditionally the stronger sex, much more decisive, self-reliant and resourceful as long as he remained unmarried (and correspondingly aloof), it was the woman who held sway as soon as the matrimonial knot was tied. "The difference between what, for lack of a better name, may be called the 'premarital' and the 'postmarital' personality," Saenger states, "appears in a minor degree to be expressed in symbolic form. While 86 per cent of the single men in the adventure strips are taller than their female partners, only 50 per cent of the married men are bigger than their wives, and 42 per cent are shorter than their spouses . . . Men lose strength as well as height after marriage. Most of the single men in the adventure strip are above average and sometimes of

Russell Patterson, Sunday supplement illustration. Although this was not, strictly speaking, a comic strip, it appeared in many newspaper Sunday supplements. Patterson's depiction of women as ethereal, almost unreachable, creatures influenced most later realistic newspaper strips.

super-natural strength, while the proportion of strong men is much smaller among married men." Which only served to bring forth the ineluctable conclusion: "Love is dangerous because it leads to marriage, a situation in which, as we have seen, men lose their strength. They can preserve their strength only by running away from women, who interfere with the real tasks in life, the seeking and pursuing of adventure." (This viewpoint can hardly be regarded as new, or exclusive to the comics: it is reflected in heroic literature from the **Old Testament** and the **Iliad** to the medieval novels of chivalry and contemporary popular fiction; on the level of formal thought this *caveat* found its most eloquent exposition in some of the writings of Schopenhauer and Nietzsche.)

Saenger's findings were reinforced some years later by some of the conclusions of a study published in 1963 by Francis E. Barcus ("The World of Sunday Comics"). Analyzing the Sunday comics appearing in the Hearst-controlled *Puck: The Comic Weekly* and in three Boston newspapers for the years 1943, 1948, 1953 and 1958, Barcus found that the world of comics is predominantly a male-populated world: "Omitting the animal characters, one finds that over two-thirds (72 per cent) of the humans are male. Males are much more often inclined to be older than are females. Men are also more likely to be

Charles Voight, sketches for "Betty." Betty was one of the very first glamor girls of the comics and Voight never tired of picturing her face fro all possible angles.

single than are women. Whereas males are almost equally distributed in the very young and the very old age brackets, a much larger percentage of males (48 per cent) are 'middle age' than are females (29 per cent)."

According to Barcus there is an even greater dichotomy between single and married persons than Saenger suspected. From his survey of 632 leading characters (out of 302 different comic strips), Barcus avers that men lose their ambitions after marriage while women, in contrast, acquire (or further) a thirst for power once they get married. While single men tend to be tall and handsome, married men turn out to be short, portly and bald; married women are often taller than their husbands, but they are also fatter and uglier than their single sisters.

Writing in the catalogue to an exhibition of comic art which took place in Rapallo, Italy, in 1976 (part of which was devoted to the theme "Woman in the Comics"), Chantal Mareuil, a French university teacher, elaborated further on the Barcus survey. Classifying what she deemed to be the most popular strips in American newspapers of 1974 into "masculine" (in which the leading role is played by a man), "feminine" (those whose protagonist is a woman), and "co-equal" (in which a couple or a family is given preeminence), Ms. Mareuil found

Sals Bostwick, "Hello Hattie." This was one among the multitude of girl strips that were a staple of the 1920's. © King Features Syndicate.

that, out of a total of 27 strips, six were "feminine," six "co-equal" and 13 "masculine" (two of the strips studied did not fit into any of these categories).

Contrasting what she found out to be the most popular women characters of the 1970's (Lucy of *Peanuts*, Broom-Hilda, Blondie, Flo of *Andy Capp* and Joanie Caucus of *Doonesbury*) with the favorites of the 1950's (Juliet Jones, Mary Worth, Daisy Mae and June of *Rex Morgan*), Ms. Mareuil concluded on a hopeful note: "The favorite women of 1974 are, on the whole, less attractive, and they still enjoy neither a successful career nor an exciting life, but all five share one thing in common: *They are no longer defeated women* . . . And that is an improvement!"

One has to admire Ms. Mareuil's self-assurance and sweeping generalizations. But was Blondie any more defeated in 1954 than she was in 1974? and is Flo (who is English, incidentally, and not American) really more assertive today than Juliet Jones (who got herself elected mayor of her town) was in the 1950's? Ms. Mareuil is guilty here of an error unfortunately common to many feminists bent on making their point, that of believing that her insight as a woman could substitute for a thorough knowledge of the subject.

It took another woman writing in the same publication, Maria-Grazia Perini, editorial head of Editoriale Corno (one of the largest publishers of comics in Italy), to place the subject in a more cogent perspective. ". . . It is obvious that woman was, for centuries, the image 'willed' by

Gladys Parker, "Mopsy." Among the rare women cartoonists who worked consistently in the comic strip idiom, Gladys Parker was one of the most prolific: she specialized in girl strips, of which "Mopsy" was one. © Associated Newspapers.

George McManus, "Bringing Up Father." McManus was a great admirer of the feminine figure, and he populated his strips with bevies of pretty girls, as in this example. © King Features Syndicate.

man, and had therefore to carry a burden of falseness and hypocrisy that has almost become congenital to her," stated Ms. Perini, adding more to the point that, "in the comics the emancipation of women is seen through special lenses: those of sex and violence. Aside from some scattered exceptions, such as **Tiffany Jones, Brenda Starr, Connie** . . ."

That the image of woman projected by the comics (and, in a wider perspective, by all popular arts) was one created by men in order to satisfy specific male needs is of course the most grievous, as well as the most valid, objection leveled at the medium by female critics. That women have much to deplore (as well as a few things to cheer about) in the comics is obvious to anyone with more than passing interest in

Roy Crane, "Wash Tubbs." Roy Crane was another cartoonist who delighted in picturing feminine beauty. © NEA Service.

the subject. Some of the examples in this book will, no doubt, provide endless grist for feminist mills. There is also no question that some comics have catered to specific male sexual fantasies: one glaring example is that of several lines of comic books published in the late 1940's and early 1950's depicting women (usually in weird costumes) in situations of an undeniable sado-masochistic nature. The standard-bearer of this group of comics (dubbed "good girl art" by aficionados of the genre) was the over-endowed, ruthless Phantom Lady. In recent times there is the rash of pornographic comics flourishing in the United States, Western Europe, Japan, and elsewhere.

It would be foolish to see in all this the evidence of a deliberate male conspiracy. It is a hard fact that comic strips and comic book artists are, and have always been, men to an overwhelming extent. Women have never amounted to more than five per cent of the total roll of cartoonists at any given time (a checklist of women comic artists can be found at the end of the volume). Writing in that same Rapallo show catalogue, Mort Walker declared that, "in trying to assemble an exhibition of women cartoonists, the Museum of Cartoon Arts produced a paucity. Out of the thousands of cartoonists in our collection, fewer than twenty are women . . ." When the time comes to

try and explain this sorry state of affairs there is usually a breakdown in communication. During a recent symposium on cartoon and humor held at the New School for Social Research in New York City, when the question of female under-representation in the cartoon field came up the hall was alive with debate and invective. The art editor of one magazine bluntly stated that aspiring women cartoonists simply didn't cut the mustard, while a number of those same aspiring women cartoonists present in the room vehemently screamed discrimination, sexism and worse—hardly an enlightening exchange of opinions.

There can be no doubt that most editors discriminated against women in the past, as **Brenda Starr** creator Dale Messick bitterly recalled: "It was always the same story. Editors couldn't believe I could draw because I was a woman"; and there is little doubt that quite a few still do, despite disclaimers to the contrary. Yet, while women should certainly be given the same chance as men in this field as well as any other, as a matter of fairness and right, the mere presence of more women cartoonists would not, in my view, lead to any appreciable improvement in the image of women in the comics. (It is naive to believe that female cartoonists would be motivated by nobler goals than male cartoonists, just as it was childish to assume that

Matt Baker, "Phantom Lady." "Phantom Lady" was the epitome of the so-called "good girl" comics which flourished in the late 1940's and early 1950's. © Fox Features Syndicate.

female politicians would be prompted by loftier ideals than male politicians, as recent history has clearly shown.)

Furthermore the record does not look good. After all, woman cartoonist Gladys Parker was as guilty of perpetuating a female stereotype in her comic strip, **Flapper Fanny,** as any of her male counterparts, while Dale Messick's Brenda Starr does not appear measurably more liberated than Stan Drake's Juliet Jones or Leonard Starr's Mary Perkins. On the other hand, the two women characters most widely respected by women, Sheena and Wonder Woman, have been created and nurtured exclusively by men.

The world of comics is unquestionably male-dominated because on the one hand society at large is unquestionably male-dominated, and on the other hand the public of the comics is unquestionably male-dominated. (Study after study has borne the fact out; furthermore one has only to visit one of the innumerable comic conventions taking place all around the country to see for oneself that most of the attendance is male, as are most of the organizers and speakers.)

While a discussion of the first point does not fall within the purview of this study, on the second point it would serve the cause of women (and that of comics) well to have more women participating in discussions and attending meetings and going to conventions — as they are increasingly doing. The comics are an important communication medium, as well as an original art form, and they deserve as much interest and scrutiny as movies, television and books. Not only does the field need more women cartoonists and editors, it also cries out for more women historians, critics and scholars. Only in this way will the comics come to reflect more accurately the concerns and image of women.

To that end I offer my own modest contribution: a visual and textual record of 80 years of feminine representation and misrepresentation in the comics . . .

Koo Kojima, comic book illustration. In recent times eroticism has become a hallmark of comics around the world. Here is a fine example from Japan. © Koo Kojima.

SALLIE SNOOKS ~ STENOGRAPHER

Sallie Snooks, Dink Shannon ("Sallie Snooks, Stenographer"). This is probably the earliest example of a working girl in the comics. The strip, started in 1907, was however an isolated phenomenon. Sallie was lost among the housewives populating the features around her, and spawned no immediate imitator. "Sallie Snooks, Stenographer" lasted only a few years and has remained in total obscurity to this day. The theme was picked up again a decade later and much more successfully developed in Hayward's "Somebody's Stenog."

THE FIRST DRAFT 1897-1910

In the beginning the world of comics was dark. No vernal, bright feminine presence was there to illuminate the night, and chaos reigned supreme. Slum kids were forever engaged in bashing one another over the head; cute animals cavorted over the landscape; and all manner of low-class, low-life characters skulked around in their incessant efforts to avoid work, domesticity and a regular bath.

The few—very few—girls to appear in the early comics were, like the stupidly grinning child-shrews in **The Yellow Kid,** made to appear as unsavory and unappealing as their male counterparts. Even more than a male society, this was a sexless society, and the stereotypic female role was that represented by Mamma Katzenjammer, always busy cooking, washing and cleaning for her two ungrateful offspring. Not even a hint of sexuality was allowed to enter: Der Captain (who many think is Die Mamma's husband) was in fact a shipwrecked sailor taken in by Die Mamma as a boarder. Nor is there any record of Mamma Katzenjammer ever mentioning the father of her twins: like Topsy, who just grew, the Kids just happened.

This picture was to change somewhat with the arrival of R. F. Outcault's **Buster Brown** (1902). Not only was there a married couple of normal appearance and respectable demeanor introduced into the strip (wife still attractive, husband quietly distinguished), but in the person of Buster's piquant companion in mischief, a brunette named Mary Jane, Outcault introduced a precocious vamp of the species that the French call **ingénue perverse** (a type that the great French novelist Colette was delineating in her famous **Claudine** series of novels around the same time). There always was, it seems to me, an underground current of childhood sexuality running through this strip, a current that would sometimes surface, as in the episode in which Buster Brown, pinned down to the ground by two giggling schoolgirls, is made the unwilling object of a kissing contest.

Mary-Jane, precocious as she might have been, was still only a very young girl, as also was Madge, the Magician's Daughter, who, for all the tricks she played on her unsuspecting playmates, still did not come up to the stature of a Circe (though she **did**, at one point, change the boys into swine). On the other hand the Princess of Slumberland (in McCay's **Little Nemo**) was already a young adult: wistful and distant, as befits a king's daughter, she could also be tender and vulnerable; under her regal manner, her sumptuous dresses and her proud, little face enhanced by dark locks, she hid a longing whose cause can only be guessed at. It was this longing that prompted King Morpheus, her father, to summon Little Nemo to Slumberland as a playmate for his daughter. The Princess (whose name we never learn) can thus be regarded as the first genuine heroine of the comics.

The comics, in the meantime, were growing up, and so were the characters they depicted. The cheery, irrepressible kids of the early years were steadily giving way to protagonists of more mature years, though usually not of more mature minds. After years of traveling the roads alone, Happy Hooligan, F.B. Opper's tin-can-hatted little tramp, was at last to meet love in the person of pert, demure Suzanne. F.M. Howarth's Leander courted his faithful Lulu from the start in 1903 and, in spite of mishap piled upon ludicrous mishap, finally managed to marry her; while Hairbreadth Harry and his arch-rival, top-hatted, fiendish Rudolph Rassendale, were forever battling it out over Belinda Blinks, "the beautiful boilermaker."

What all these girls had in common was an acceptance of their social role as the weaker sex. Suzanne would wait patiently for Happy, hoping that her father would relent in his opposition to her marrying the tramp; Lulu would be nearly as passive in spite of her suitor's nefarious schemes; while Belinda, whether in the clutches of the despicable Rudolph, or facing some equally hideous peril, would call out for the miraculous intervention of her hero (who always managed to arrive in the nick of time). What was uppermost in each girl's mind was marriage, and once she had accepted what could pass for a formal engagement of sorts, it would have seemed sacrilegious to choose a different (and easier) path, even in the face of the most outrageous provocations.

In Gustave Verbeck's weird strip, **The Upside Downs of Little Lady Lovekins and Old Man Muffaroo**, the female character displays the same passive behavior in relation to Old Man Muffaroo (a strictly non-romantic attachment); she clings to the male for succor and protection, despite the fact that Muffaroo is just as terrified as she by the numerous perils they encounter.

Another facet of the feminine mystique was in evidence in Gene Carr's **Lady Bountiful**. The title character, a rather young and attractive-looking woman, is a modern incarnation of the fairy godmothers of old. She bestows upon her charges, an unruly lot of unkempt urchins, a multitude of quite undeserved goodies, and displays the utmost patience, forbearance and understanding. She quite obviously presents the reader with the reassurance of a mother-image, while at the same time maintaining both a picture of feminine attractiveness and an aura of sexual innocence, a psychological projection of every man's fantasy about motherhood.

The female half of George McManus's **The Newlyweds** stands at the opposite end of the spectrum. Physically modelled after the then-fashionable "Gibson girl" (a feminine type to which McManus was to remain faithful throughout his long career) she seems to enjoy a happy sex life. While her existence (and that of her husband) would, on the surface, seem to revolve around their obnoxious baby whom she outrageously pampers and spoils, it is clear that her fixation stems not from a sense of maternal duty, but from the genuine affection she feels toward the child's father. While the baby goes on enjoying his idiotic whims, the Newlyweds freely coo in each other's arms ("isn't he adorable, dearie?", "the very image of his mother, precious"), in an unabashed display of conjugal bliss. In his knowing and loving treatment of sex McManus proved to be, as in so many other fields, a groundbreaker.

In the first ten years of the century the comics reflected with rather astonishing accuracy the slowly changing status of woman in the post-Victorian society of urban America, from her almost complete relegation to the shadow of man, to her first steps into a more assertive role. In this respect, as in many others, the comics proved to be a barometer closely attuned to the temper of the times.

5. "Aha! Dey are making a water works yet-"

6. ! ! ? ! !

Mamma Katzenjammer, Rudolph Dirks ("The Katzenjammer Kids"). The first woman to hold a permanent role in any comic strip, Die Mamma (or Mama, both spellings were used) ran true to the stereotype of the German **hausfrau:** she was always busy cooking, dusting, cleaning and washing. Her main task, however, was to keep a loving, if wary, eye on her progeny, the diabolical Hans and Fritz. Mamma Katzenjammer had dreams of one day seeing her "liddle anchels" becoming President and Vice-President, yet this did not deter her from punishing the twins after they had overstepped the bounds of her tolerance (which they invariably managed to do). Started in 1897, "The Katzenjammer Kids" is still being published today, making it the longest-running comic strip in existence.

Mary-Jane, Richard Felton Outcault ("Buster Brown"). The dark-haired Mary-Jane was as much of a hellion as her constant companion in mischief, Buster Brown. Her angelic face hid a devilish mind, while the large ribbon in her hair and her black stockings contributed to her image as a precocious vamp—a role she filled with relish by letting her companion suffer punishment for their jointly-perpetrated pranks. Mary-Jane pursued her exploits for almost a quarter of a century, from 1902 (when the "Buster Brown" strip was originated) to 1926, the year of its demise.

The Princess of Slumberland, Winsor McCay ("Little Nemo in Slumberland"). The black-tressed Princess presented an image of youthful poise, grace and charm in the weird kingdom of Slumberland. While she was often upstaged by the shenanigans of Flip the dwarf and Impy the cannibal, she nonetheless remained a principal figure in both "Little Nemo" (1905–1911) and its sequel "In the World of Wonderful Dreams" (1911–1914), as well as in the second version of "Little Nemo" (1924–1927).

Suzanne, Frederick Burr Opper ("Happy Hooligan"). In the midst of all his misadventures the hapless Happy found time to court (sometimes with devouring ardor) the pert Suzanne. Like another famous tramp, Charlie Chaplin, he managed to win her in the end. Suzanne herself was a model of acidulous attractiveness, and did not always conform to her role of dutiful daughter. The adventures of Suzanne and Happy filled the comic pages from 1900 to 1932. © the Star Company.

LITTLE NEMO IN SLUMBERLAND
FLIP IS FURIOUS, ISN'T HE NEMO?
I DON'T BLAME HIM. I'D BE MADDER THAN HE.
THERE'S NO ONE CAN SQUIRT INK IN MY FACE AND GET AWAY WITH IT. SEE?
THAT OLD WITCH WILL NEVER DRIVE HIM OUT OF SLUMBERLAND
THEN WHY DOESN'T SHE GIVE IT UP AND LEAVE HIM ALONE?
YOU ARE A SWEET LITTLE GIRL ONE MINUTE AND AN OLD WITCH THE NEXT
YOU CAN'T FOOL ME I SAW YOU DO IT!
HE WILL NOT BE ABLE TO CATCH HER, SO LET US GO ON TO THE SNOW PALACE
I'M A FOXY KID IF I DO SAY IT AND NO WITCH CAN FOOL ME
AW! FLIP! LET HER GO! MAYBE SHE DIDN'T DO IT.
LOOK AT THAT TREE! OH! OH!
THE WITCH IS DOING THAT, BUT IT WON'T SCARE FLIP.
I DON'T LIKE THAT WITCH. I WISH SHE WOULD GO HOME.
WE'LL GO TO THE ICE AND SNOW PALACE. HE WILL FOLLOW
DO YOU KNOW, I THINK THAT BOY IS UP AGAIN? I BELIEVE I HEAR HIM. - NEMO! GET BACK INTO BED!
WINSOR McCAY
COPYRIGHT, 1907, BY THE NEW YORK HERALD CO.

2. CHARLEY ONTHESPOT: "Why, certainly the ice is safe."
LIEUTENANT SHARPNELL: "Of course it is. WE know."
LULU: "Then I am going, Leander. I don't believe you want to skate."
LEANDER: "Lulu, you shall NOT go You shall not risk your life."

Lulu, F.M. Howarth ("Lulu and Leander"). Lulu was a much-courted young girl who remained faithful to her one love, the slick-haired, fast-talking Leander, in spite of hot competition from such worthwhile rivals as Lieutenant Shrapnell and Charley Onthespot. All the characters had the typically Howarthian oversized head. The strip (which did not use balloons, but had a narrative running beneath the pictures) ran from 1903 to 1906.

Belinda Blinks, Charles William Kahles ("Hairbreadth Harry"). Belinda Blinks, "the beautiful boilermaker," may be termed the first heroine of the comics. She encountered perils upon untold perils at the hands of the snarling, top-hatted stage villain, Rudolph Rassendale, before being rescued (in the nick of time, of course!) by her handsome boyfriend-hero, "Hairbreadth" Harry Hollingsworth.

Little Lady Lovekins, Gustave Verbeck ("The Upside Downs of Little Lady Lovekins and Old Man Muffaroo"). In Verbeck's strip, the little lady in question appeared more often than not, as an amorphous blob, since the artist was more interested in the strip's novel narrative technique (which consisted of turning the feature upside down to read further) than in its characters. The strip enjoyed a short life-span (from 1903 to 1905).

Lady Bountiful, Gene Carr. Gene Carr created "Lady Bountiful" for the New York Herald in 1904. The title character (always addressed as "Lady Bountiful") was in the beginning endowed with fairy-like faculties; later she turned into a regular young woman of average capabilities whose best intentions always boomeranged against her. The strip was popular enough, and continued well into the 1930's.

Mrs. Newlywed, George McManus ("The Newlyweds and their only child"). Next to "Bringing Up Father," McManus's best known and most enduring creation, "The Newlyweds and Their Baby" started in 1904 in the New York World; when McManus transferred to the Hearst organization in 1912 he took the feature with him, renaming it "Their Only Child." (The original "Newlyweds," meantime, was being continued by Albert Carmichael.) In the 1940's and 1950's the revived feature was known as "Snookums" (Snookums was the name of the Newlyweds' obnoxious offspring). Mrs. Newlywed (like her husband she had no known first name) was the embodiment of the "Gibson girl"; well-coiffed, handsomely dressed and exquisitely-mannered, she was to display her somewhat vacuous good looks for almost a half-century.

Bécassine, Caumery (Maurice Languereau) and J.P. Pinchon. In 1905 the most famous heroine of the early European comics made her appearance: she was the little Breton maid nicknamed Bécassine (bird brain) by her companions. Despite her blunders she pursued her eventful career through two world wars and countless upheavals. The feature is still in existence today, after having charmed four generations of young French readers since its inception. © Gauthier-Languereau.

Fluffy Ruffles, Wallace Morgan. For two years 1907–1909), Fluffy Ruffles presented to the readers of the New York Herald (and of the other papers carrying Herald features) the ideal image of the American girl, so stunningly beautiful that her effect on the men she encountered was nothing short of devastating. Fluffy's lightly humorous attempts at holding one job after another (attempts all doomed to failure because of her disruptive effect on male co-workers) formed the theme of this weekly feature.

Madge the Magician's Daughter, W.O. Wilson. Madge was the female equivalent of the Sorcerer's Apprentice. Every time she would take hold of her father's magic wand she would use it to some unwholesome purpose. "Madge" ran for several years in a number of newspapers, from approximately 1905 to 1910.

Constance, Clare Briggs ("Danny Dreamer"). The dream was a universal theme of comic strips of the times. The misnamed Constance was the dream object of the title character. Fickle, coquettish and heartless, she was a typical **ingenue perverse** of the funnies. "Danny Dreamer" ran from 1907 to 1914.

Phyllis, Gene Carr. Phyllis (who made her appearance in 1902) was the epitome of comic-strip female characters: fat, homely and dim-witted, she was seen as an object of derision rather than a sex symbol.

Miss Peachtree, Ed Carey ("Simon Simple"). Ed Carey's Simon Simple was a clownish simpleton whose attempts at courting the lovely Miss Peachtree always ended in disaster. The charming lass formed an incongruous contrast to the nondescript Simon.

Mamma, Penny Ross ("Mamma's Angel Child"). "Mamma's Angel Child" was created in the same year (1904) and with the same theme as "The Newlyweds." If anything the "angel child" was even more obnoxious than Snookums. The strip was best noted, however, for Mamma's stylish clothes and fashions. (In spite of the feminine consonance of the artist's name, Penny Ross was a certified male.)

A PLACE OF ONE'S OWN 1910-1919

The 1910's marked the time when women came into their own—albeit to a limited extent—in the funny papers. While the population of the comic pages remained predominantly male with married women still tied to the old stereotypes of either nagging harridan (Maggie of **Bringing Up Father**) or paragon of domesticity (Min of **The Gumps**), young women, especially unmarried girls, were beginning to assert personalities of their own, and to take their place, some with discretion, others with **éclat**, in this male-oriented society.

Of all the leading cartoonists George McManus was undoubtedly the decade's greatest contributor to feminine iconography. McManus is best remembered for his portrayal of the overbearing Maggie and her husband the long-suffering Jiggs, but as an unabashed admirer of the female figure, McManus created two of the most lovely-looking girls of the comics: Rosie (of **Rosie's Beau**) and Nora (Maggie and Jiggs's daughter in **Bringing Up Father**). They are more noted, however, for their decorative qualities, the shapeliness of their legs, and the style of their clothes, than for their intellectual quotient: Rosie endlessly swoons over her beau Archibald's trite love declarations, while Nora perennially falls for aristocratic scions of Europe who are either paupers or fakes.

Yet McManus's lovelies shine with special brightness, caressed as they are by the artist's loving pen and understanding complicity. McManus delights in picturing the girls in the most languid and alluring poses, and while these creatures may strike us as foolish or vain, they are never made to appear ridiculous. McManus was nothing if not a male chauvinist (albeit an inspired one): his female characters are either empty-headed sex objects or forbidding, repellent battleaxes. He died, apparently unrepentant, in 1954; yet one wonders what would have happened to his creations had he managed to survive into the woman's liberation era.

The tradition pioneered by Belinda Blinks in **Hairbreadth Harry** received further impetus from Harry Hershfield's heroine Rosamond in the Hearst-distributed **Desperate Desmond.** Like Belinda, Rosamond was involved in the fierce tug-of-war between her two rival suitors, her fiancé Claude Eclair and the dastardly villain, Desperate Desmond (for whom, characteristically, the strip was named). Rosamond underwent all of the blood-curdling ordeals which mark the true-to-form comic strip heroine (tied to railroad tracks, dangling from the Brooklyn Bridge, engulfed by a raging blaze); the switch was that she managed to save her somewhat dull-witted lover from peril as often as he rescued her. Her feats of daring (which started in 1910) grew more and more outlandish and far-fetched, and it is only legitimate to assume that her cliff-hanging adventures must have inspired, at least by example, the screen exploits of such female stalwarts as Kathryn Williams in **The Adventures of Kathryn** (1913) and, even more strikingly, those of Pearl White in **The Perils of Pauline** (1914) which, not coincidentally, was financed by the aforementioned Hearst.

While in this instance (as in a number of others) the comics had clearly been ahead of the movies, the film serials were in turn to inspire the comics into such wild take-offs as **Haphazard Helen**, Billy De Beck's early comic strip attempt, an outrageous spoof on yet another screen cliff-hanger of the times, **The Hazards of Helen.**

More traditional female types also came to the fore in the comics of the decade, such as the grasping wife in **Pa's Son-in-Law,** and (to balance things out) Abie's understanding, wise and helpful girl friend (and later wife), Reba Mine Gold Pearlman, of **Abie the Agent,** a later Hershfield creation.

The most idiosyncratic, opinionated and self-assertive girl of the time appeared only toward the end of the decade (in 1919 precisely) in E. C. Segar's comic confection, **Thimble Theater**: she was Olive Oyl, the surly female rosebud of the Oyl family. The comic love affair between Olive and her big-nosed boyfriend, Harold Ham Gravy, provided the crux of the action for a while, but soon Olive took off after bigger game. Along with her irascible nincompoop of a brother, Castor, she would embark on a multitude of undertakings, most of them harebrained, and end up doing most of the work, however protestingly. With her non-descript face perched atop her scrawny figure, she presented a sorry example of womanhood, but her indomitable spirit and fierce individuality made her a force to reckon with, and she easily eclipsed her male acolytes, at least until she finally met her match at the end of 10 love-starved years (but this will be recounted in a later chapter).

Olive Oyl could be said to have been a working girl of sorts, but to another, more obscure cartoonist, A. E. Hayward, belongs the distinction of having created the first career girl of the comics, in a strip called **Somebody's Stenog**. Born of the manpower shortage of WW I this epitome of office girls seemed to spend more time on personal pursuits than on office work, a tradition that would be perpetuated in the hordes of working girl strips to come. Yet she undisputably helped break new ground in the comics: for the first time there was a woman who was seen as an independent person, tied to neither parents nor husband, and making her way in the world through work, charm, ingenuity, and more than a little nerve.

Interesting (and sometimes remarkable) as the previous female characters might have been they all pale a little before the most enduring female creation of the decade, a cool blonde beauty (later turned into a brunette, for some inexplicable reason) by the name of Polly. But, blonde or brunette, as Coulton Waugh wrote, "Polly is historically important because she is the first of a type . . . bulging brow, tiny nose and mouth, huge, deep-set eyes. Add long, well displayed legs . . . and you have Polly, a perfect picture of an upstanding, American girl-goddess."

This girl-goddess first appeared in 1912 and was named by Cliff Sterrett, her creator (who had served his apprenticeship of drawing girls in **For This We Have Daughters?**), Positive Polly, in a strip of that title (later changed to the better-known **Polly and Her Pals**). Although Polly's mild flirtations with her collegiate suitors were slight, and her triumphs over her parents, the redoubtable Maw and the hapless Paw Perkins, stereotypical, she set a pattern, established a mood. All the later heroines of the 1920's, whether serious-minded or frivolous, would owe something to Polly's seductively aloof manner and headstrong impulsiveness.

Maggie, George McManus ("Bringing Up Father"). The redoubtable Maggie appeared in 1913, as the shrewish and social-climbing wife of the happy-go-lucky Jiggs. Always ready with the crushing epithet or the flying rolling pin, she personifies to millions of Americans the overbearing and dominating wife. Her face may be homely, but she keeps a trim figure, and her clothes are always up to fashion. Maggie is today as active and aggressive as ever, 23 years after her creator's death. © King Features Syndicate.

Nora, George McManus ("Bringing Up Father"). Maggie and Jiggs's stunningly beautiful daughter, Nora is a lovely contrast to her mother's homeliness and pugnacity. Indolent and mannered, she only has thoughts of stylish clothes, fashionable parties and aristocratic suitors (she was eventually to marry an English lord). © King Features Syndicate.

Rosie, George McManus ("Rosie's Beau"). Rosie was a typical McManus beauty, courted by a fat double-chinned office worker named Archibald. The comical Archibald's amorous ardors never grew tiresome to the lovely and big-hearted Rosie (like most McManus lovelies, Rosie was as short on brains as she was long on looks). "Rosie's Beau" ran (with some interruptions) from 1916 to 1944.

Rosamond, Harry Hershfield ("Desperate Desmond"). Rosamond pioneered in the funnies the tradition of the spunky and resourceful heroine always threatened by some deadly peril. Caught between her pure-hearted (but somewhat clumsy) fiancé, Claude Eclair, and her dastardly pursuer, the villainous Desperate Desmond, she often managed to make fools of them both. "Desperate Desmond" unfolded its merry tapestry of outrageous goings-on for over two years, from 1910 to 1912. © International Feature Service.

Ma, C.H. Wellington ("Pa's Son-in-Law"). The stereotype of the overbearing wife was perpetuated in a great number of American comic strips of the second decade of the century. In addition to Maggie there were countless other wives who delighted in cowing their hopelessly hen-pecked husbands, such as the towering Ma of "Pa's Son-in-Law." (The feature started in the mid-1910's as a take-off on the Charlie Chaplin craze, but later evolved into a classic bickering-couple strip.) © N.Y. Tribune.

Reba Mine Gold Pearlman, Harry Hershfield ("Abie the Agent"). Reba was Abie Kabibble's long-suffering girlfriend. When she later married him she did not turn into an insufferable battleaxe as so many of her comic strip sisters, but continued to provide the impractical Abie with understanding, solace and wise (but always gentle) motherly advice. "Abie the Agent" was Hershfield's most popular strip, lasting from 1914 until the late 1930's.

Little Mary Mixup, Robert Moore Brinkerhoff. Conceived in 1917, little Mary was a devilish blonde hellion whose pranks belied her innocent mien. She later grew up and even joined the fight against the Nazis during WW II. She is best remembered, however, for the youthful spirits and falsely angelic manners she displayed in her earlier life.

Cinderella Peggy, H.A. MacGill. Variations on the Cinderella theme were prevalent in the course of the decade. In "Cinderella Peggy" the title heroine was usually able to fob off her assigned chores on eager suitors. H.A. MacGill (of "The Hall Room Boys" fame) was also the author of another short-lived girl strip of the period, "Hazel the Heartbreaker."

Mabel, Charles Voight ("Petey"). Voight had started his comic strip career as early as 1908 with "Petey Dink," an early effort at humor. When Voight later joined the New York Tribune, his strip became simply "Petey," and soon Uncle Petey found himself upstaged by the bevy of young beauties that were continually strewn in his path. Mabel, Petey's favorite niece, was one of the most stunning of Voight's many female creations. © N.Y. Tribune.

Polly, Cliff Sterrett ("Polly and Her Pals"). The best-known among early comic strip heroines, Polly made her debut as "Positive Polly" in 1912. She immediately established a pattern, that of the attractive, somewhat cool and aloof unmarried girl. The readers were responsive, if sometimes puzzled by Polly's changeable hair color (Sterrett portrayed her alternately as a blonde and a brunette). But, whatever shade were her tresses, she always managed to shine brightly in the midst of all the shenanigans going on around her. Comic historians have usually fawned over her charms. Coulton Waugh called her an "American girl-goddess," and Stephen Becker rhapsodized: "Polly is a doll. She is the saucer-eyed, snub-nosed, curly-haired, long-legged descendant of the healthy beauties of the 1890s." Others have been hardly less enthusiastic, and their praise has earned Polly special star status among comic strip heroines.

"Polly and Her Pals" was a success from the beginning, and it ended only with the retirement of Sterrett in 1958.

Min Gump, Sidney Smith ("The Gumps"). A plain but determined housewife with redoubtable powers of persuasion, Minerva (Min) Gump was the matriarch of the Gump clan. Even the loud-mouthed Andy, her husband, usually ended up following her homespun admonitions, however much he might at first resist her wifely advice. She symbolized the "family brains" (as well as its conscience) and used her wits rather than a crude rolling pin, to assert her dominance. Immensely popular from the start (in 1917), "The Gumps" sharply declined, following Smith's death in 1935, and folded in 1959. © Chicago Tribune-New York News Syndicate.

Olive Oyl, E.C. Segar ("Thimble Theater"). This fearless symbol of spinsterhood made her first appearance in 1919. Lending help and support to her brother Castor's harebrained get-rich-quick schemes (and only getting disgusted rebuffs as her reward) Olive would in turn take out her anger on her dim-witted boyfriend, the banana-nosed Harold Ham Gravy—always dreaming in the meantime of the dashing Prince Charming who would sweep her off her feet. © King Features Syndicate.

Cinderella Suze, Jack Callahan. Another twist on the old Cinderella tale was provided by Jack Callahan. In this one Cinderella Suze manages to turn the tables on her two snickering stepsisters and their overbearing mother thanks to her good looks and demure manner. "Cinderella Suze" ran roughly from 1914 to 1918.

The Stenog, A.E. Hayward ("Somebody's Stenog"). Hayward ushered in the tradition of working-girl strips with "Somebody's Stenog," which he created around 1917 (and which lasted into the 1940's). The blonde and attractive heroine (whose name was never disclosed during all those years) displayed her charms in a variety of settings besides her office. She also displayed brains in addition to looks, another startling departure from comic strip tradition. © Ledger Syndicate.

WORKING GIRLS AND FLAPPERS 1920-1929

1920 was a momentous year in the history of women's rights in the United States: with the adoption of the 19th amendment to the Constitution women finally won the right to vote, after years of lobbying and agitation. The effect must have been as electrifying on comic strip artists as it was on the country at large: in a matter of a few years women started populating the strips in ever-increasing numbers, as well as in ever more visible roles (although, by and large, men still outnumbered women in the comic pages by a wide margin). More importantly, many new strips starred a woman as the title character: in short order there appeared Martin Branner's **Winnie Winkle** (1920), Russ Westover's **Tillie the Toiler** (1921), Edgar Martin's **Boots and Her Buddies** (1924), Plumb and Conselman's **Ella Cinders** (1925), Frank Godwin's **Connie** (1927), as well as **Fritzi Ritz, Dumb Dora, Jane Arden, Dixie Dugan,** and many others, a fitting tribute to American women's enhanced status as well as to their growing economic and political power.

This economic power had been brought out, in great part, by the increasing numbers of women who now joined America's work force. As stated in the historical introduction to **The World Encyclopedia of Comics**: "The family-type comics were created to attract a female readership, and nowhere was this as apparent as in the so-called girl strips. Aimed particularly at the growing number of working girls, they presented a flattering self-picture of independence, attractiveness (even glamour) and poise, the image of self-reliance mixed with charm."

The quintessential representation of the working girl in the comics is without a doubt that of Winnie Winkle, dubbed "the breadwinner" in the early days of the strip: in her dealings with her parents and her suitors Winnie displays the cool aplomb and efficient manner of the true professional (though she is often upstaged and sometimes outsmarted by her young brother Perry). The **Winnie Winkle** strip, however, did not concentrate on Winnie's working routine, but on her romances, her dreams, and her efforts to achieve her place in the world.

The pattern set by **Winnie Winkle** was firmly established by **Tillie the Toiler.** To pretend that Tillie was toiling at her job (as secretary and part-time model in the fashion salon of Mr. Simpkins) was somehow misleading (or perhaps ironic) since she managed to fob off most of her office work on her hapless shrimp of a suitor, the benumbed Mac, all the better to pursue every eligible bachelor in and out of the office.

Winnie and Tillie were office girls, and in the early 1920's that was the best position to which most working girls could aspire. In the second half of the decade new horizons seemed to open up. Jane Arden was the first successful female newspaper reporter of the comics, and the first to break a pattern, in that her job, not marriage, was uppermost in her life.

Jane Arden was a serious, even sober, strip. Cartoonists, however, preferred glamor rather than real-life situations for their heroines, and this was evidenced strongly by the rash of show-business strips that proliferated all through the 1920's. Aside from such obvious come-ons as **Olly of the Movies** and **Dolly of the Follies**, other strips also featured heroines immersed in the dizzying world of entertainment. **Dixie Dugan** started life as **Show Girl**, and, as such, took place in a theater setting but the formula did not work, and Dixie had to leave her budding Broadway career early in the 1930's.

Even more fanciful was the story of Ella Cinders. As the name implies, this was a comic strip version of the Cinderella tale, in which Ella toiled for her selfish mother, the domineering Mytie Cinders, and her two step-sisters, Prissie and Lotta Pill, until, one day, she won a Hollywood contract and achieved a brilliant career in the movies. This was a common dream among millions of American girls at the time, and the comics simply embroidered upon the theme. (In the case of **Ella Cinders**, the dream was to come true within the space of one short year, when the strip was made into a film starring Coleen Moore in the title role in 1926—another of the many instances of life imitating art.)

A twist on the Hollywood syndrome was provided by Ed Wheelan who, in his **Minute Movies,** starting in 1921, imagined a cast of characters capable of handling any possible movie role. His ingenue was Hazel Dearie, a curly blonde modelled after Mary Pickford; and his vamp Blanche Rouge, inspired by Theda Bara. In a tongue-in-cheek reversal of the comic strip conventions of the times, Wheelan decided to concentrate on the girls' screen impersonations rather than on their off-screen adventures. The format allowed for a greater range of experiences and situations, and in their circuitous ways, the doubly imaginary Blanche and Hazel can be regarded as the first "liberated" girls of the comics.

In the rarified atmosphere of 1920's comic strips, college girls and "flappers" (who were indistinguishable in the eyes of a great majority of the American public, as well, apparently, as in those of most cartoonists) were even more popular than career girls. Possibly the first to arrive on the scene was Lillums Lovewell, the "queen" of **Harold Teen's** campus world, where she first appeared in 1920. She did not long remain alone. Pretty soon there were Syncopating Sue, a genuine baby of the jazz age, who owed her nickname to her enthusiasm for the charleston; Freddie the Sheik's many girl-friends (or "Shebas" in the college slang of the times), even the aptly named Hotsy-Totsy, not to mention Gladys Parker's creation, Flapper Fanny (while conceived by a woman, Fanny nonetheless ran true to the stereotype of the pretty scatterbrain, only interested in dancing, fast cars and rich boyfriends). All those strips had in common an exclusive, almost manic, preoccupation with the light, glamorous side of collegiate life.

Somewhat more subdued was Boots (of **Boots and Her Buddies**). While the spotlight was pretty much on Boots's extra-curricular activities (always innocent, in spite of hordes of suitors whom she tactfully kept at bay), some glimpses of real life were allowed into the strip, such as Boots cramming for an exam, or taking a part-time job to pay for a new dress. In her own way the title character of **Etta Kett** was almost more proper than Boots, and her private life was a model of rectitude. The curvaceous, lovely brunette never went beyond a chaste good-night kiss. This paragon of middle-class virtue kept true to her name by dispensing tips as to suitable dress and appropriate manners, thereby keeping teenagers posted on the latest fads and fashions.

One young and enterprising cartoonist even made a career out of the depiction of the frivolous young ladies of the 1920's: he was Murat (better known as "Chic") Young, who made a big hit with just such a creature in the next decade. Young actually started his cartooning career precisely in 1920, having created that year **The Affairs of Jane** (Jane was a quite innocent young girl, in spite of the implications of the strip's title). He then followed with **Beautiful Bab**, the humorous adventures of a lively blonde in a girls' school. In 1925 came his most famous creation to date, about yet another college-age girl, a brunette this time, named Dora Bell, and nicknamed Dumb Dora ("She Ain't So Dumb!"). The strip title contributed a by-word to the American language, and helped to identify a certain type of status-seeking girl (although it must be said in all fairness that Dora had her good points, and could be quite bright on occasions).

Directly descended from the girl strips of the previous decade, but different in emphasis and style were Frank Godwin's **Connie** and **Betty** by Charles Voight (who had taken over from Russ Westover). To begin with, both these artists were illustrators (not cartoonists), and the atmosphere of their strips was bathed in the creamy elegance of the slick magazines of the period. There was an air of opulence, sophistication and class about both Betty and Connie that their more high-kicking sisters did not possess. Betty was a rather languorous brunette whom Voight delighted in portraying in advantageous poses; her mind, unfortunately, did not match her looks and she was to remain a rather vacuous character throughout her life.

Connie had been patterned, in part at least, on Betty, especially in the beginning. She was blonde, and much more vivacious than Betty, but her interests were the same (parties, upper crust suitors, formal receptions, etc.). In the 1930's Connie was to evolve into one of the most admirable heroines of the comics, but in the early days of the strip she was still seen as a very young woman, carefree and fun-loving, with a strong intimation of her later poised, controlled self, and a quick, ready wit.

Captain Joseph Patterson, publisher of the **New York News**, was among the first to actively promote readership of the comics among women, and he saw to it that the comic strips distributed by his syndicate had their rightful quota of female lead characters. Thus, to Harold Gray who had come to him with a comic strip idea about an orphan boy named Andy, Patterson simply enjoined: "Put skirts on the kid and call her Little Orphan Annie." In that particular case it hardly made any difference since, with or without skirts, Gray's little orphan displays absolutely no feminine attributes. The same cannot be said of Annie's rival in the waif business, Brandon Walsh's Little Annie Rooney, whose precocious coquetry and girlish mannerisms pre-date Shirley Temple movies by a full five years.

The comic strip scene was not occupied exclusively by flappers and emancipated women: stereotypes of an earlier era were still being perpetuated. Ma Feitelbaum was an early representation of the Jewish mother, whose only concern was for her brood, the misnamed "Nize Baby," and his older brother Isidore, the bane of the family. ("Morris, not on de head!" was Ma Feitelbaum's plaintive admonition to her husband about to hit the scapegrace Isidore.) Vanilla (she of the Villains) continued a cliff-hanging tradition started in the movies by **The Perils of Pauline** and in the comics by such characters as Belinda Blinks and Rosamond of **Desperate Desmond** (it is no coincidence that **Vanilla and the Villains** was ghost-written by Harry Hershfield, the author of **Desperate Desmond**). Toots of **Toots and Casper** was a happily married young woman who, with her husband Casper formed a loving twosome, in the earlier tradition of Mr. and Mrs. Newlywed, and in sharp contrast to such bickering couples as Maggie and Jiggs, or Clare Briggs's **Mr. and Mrs.**

It is well to remember that the sudden invasion of the comics by a host of female characters was not an isolated phenomenon, but indicative of an occurence that was simultaneously taking place in all the mass-media of the time: in magazines (where romance stories became a flourishing staple), as well as in movies (with the proliferation of vamps, "it" girls and flappers). It was one more sign of the growing power of women in American society.

Winnie Winkle, Martin Branner. Dubbed "the breadwinner," Winnie Winkle made her first appearance in 1920 and is probably the best known among working girls of the funnies. She led an eventful life in and out of the office where she worked; after playing the field for a while, she got married in 1937. Her husband, however, disappeared under mysterious circumstances a few years later and, after a vain search, Winnie rediscovered the single life. Flirtatious as ever, Winnie is still able to turn many a man's head, though she now has to contend with a new rival in the person of her own daughter, Wendy.

"Winnie Winkle" is now being drawn by Max van Bibber, a former assistant to Martin Branner. Branner himself died in 1970. © Chicago Tribune-New York News Syndicate.

Tillie the Toiler, Russ Westover. Following hard on the heels of Winnie, Tillie made her entrance early in 1921. The strip followed the same pattern of office intrigue and fitful romance, with Tillie spurning the devoted but pint-sized Mac in favor of every handsome lout that happened on the scene. She finally married the long-suffering Mac in April 1959 shortly before the strip's demise. The strip's continued popularity in the 1920's and 1930's was primarily due to the fashions displayed by Tillie during her adventures. Tillie herself was a rather vain and not too interesting heroine.

Jane Arden, Monte Barrett and Russell Ross. Jane Arden was the first girl reporter to make it big in the comic pages, in spite of a bewildering succession of artists and writers. Her adventures lasted from 1928 into the late 1950's. In addition to Russell Ross, the artists who worked on the strip included Frank Ellis, Jack McGuire and Bob Schoenke.

Dixie Dugan, John Striebel and J.P. McEvoy. "Dixie Dugan" was originally called "Show Girl" when it first appeared in 1929. It was based on a best-selling novel of that title by J.P. McEvoy. As the title implied Dixie was an aspiring actress, but the formula did not work, and Dixie was moved out of her show-business setting and thrown into a unending string of romantic and professional adventures. The strip lasted into the 1960's, with an ever-decreasing readership.

Ella Cinders, Bill Conselman and Charles Plumb. Unlike Dixie Dugan, the spunky Ella Cinders made it into the movies, in spite of a freckled face and an ungainly figure. The strip itself was an amusing take-off on the Cinderella theme, and it earned well-deserved popularity soon after its inception in 1925. In the 1940's Ella's appeal began to wane, however, and the strip was finally discontinued in the 1960's. © United Feature Syndicate.

Flapper Fanny, Gladys Parker. Gladys Parker was among the relatively few successful women cartoonists. Flapper Fanny was true to the type of the empty-headed flapper, in the spirit of the 1920's, but the artist endowed her with an acidulous charm and an often disarming ingenuity that were her redeeming graces. (Gladys Parker is also the author of the later **Mopsy,** a girl strip in the same vein.) © NEA Service.

Blanche Rouge, Ed Wheelan ("Minute Movies"). Blanche Rouge was the vamp of the Wheelan studios, a position she filled with gusto. The make-believe film adventures of Blanche, Hazel and the rest of the "Minute Movies" cast (which included such wonderfully named characters as Dick Dare, Hal Fracas and Ralph McSneer) lasted from 1921 until the late 1930's.

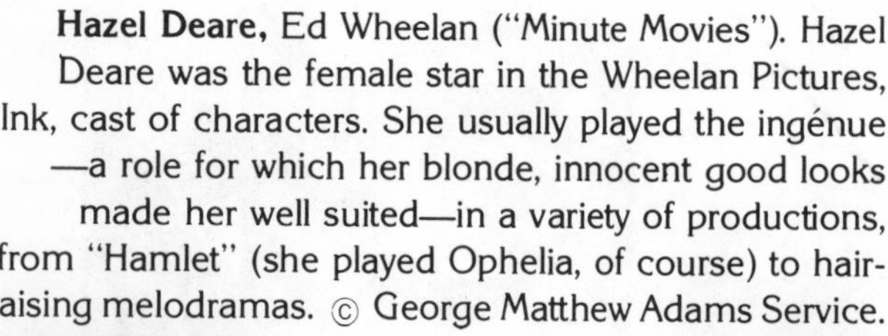

Hazel Deare, Ed Wheelan ("Minute Movies"). Hazel Deare was the female star in the Wheelan Pictures, Ink, cast of characters. She usually played the ingénue—a role for which her blonde, innocent good looks made her well suited—in a variety of productions, from "Hamlet" (she played Ophelia, of course) to hair-raising melodramas.

Lillums Lovewell, Carl Ed ("Harold Teen"). While the "Harold Teen" strip itself was first introduced in 1919 (as "The Love Life of Harold Teen"), its most noted female character did not make her appearance until the following year: she was Lillums Lovewell, the new campus queen and later Harold's steady girlfriend. Independent-minded, capricious and strong-willed, Lillums soon established the moral and trendy tone of the strip: she was the first to bob her hair, and introduced the latest slang and fashions. "Harold Teen" enjoyed wide popularity in the 1920's, but its appeal steadily declined in later years, and the strip was folded soon after the creator's death in 1959.

Dumb Dora, Murat "Chic" Young. Of quite longer duration—as well as of greater renown—was "Dumb Dora," created by Chic Young in 1925. A lively, good-looking brunette, Dora (whose nickname proved quite undeserved) kept a long roster of suitors on a string, most notably the dumpy, straw-hatted and much put-upon Rodney Ruckett. Dora's adventures were quite popular, and when Young left the strip in 1930, "Dumb Dora" was continued, first by Paul Fung, then by Bill Dwyer, until its demise in the mid-1930's. © King Features Syndicate.

Connie, Frank Godwin. The most interesting girl of the decade, Constance Kurridge was born in 1927 from the inspired pen of illustrator Frank Godwin. Called Connie by her friends (of which she had many) the svelte, blonde beauty was not at first very different from all the other cuties then filling the comic pages. Her spirit of independence and smiling determination stood her in good stead throughout the adventurous life created for her in the following decades.

Boots, Edgar Martin ("Boots and Her Buddies"). The blonde, vivacious Boots was also a campus co-ed when she first embarked on her adventures in 1924. She later went from naive adolescent to model wife to mod mother without missing a beat. Although attractively drawn, Boots alternated widely between buxom maiden and slender nymph, due to Martin's often confusing graphic style. Following the creator's death in 1960, "Boots" was continued for a number of years by Les Carroll, a former Martin assistant. © NEA Service.

Betty, Charles Voight. After Voight took over "Betty," he remade it into the model of the new, crisp style of illustrated strip. He particularly delighted in the depiction of pretty girls, Betty foremost among them, of course. The strip was much admired for its style and draftsmanship, but the goings-on were rather dull. It folded in 1943. © New York Tribune.

Little Orphan Annie, Harold Gray. Probably the most celebrated waif of American pop culture, Annie was created in 1924 by Harold Gray, who had initially intended to make her a boy. The sex change (prompted by Gray's boss, Joseph Medill Patterson) proved exceptionally beneficial, as Annie pursued her heart-rending adventures in the company of her dog, Sandy, and under the watchful protection of her adoptive father, the omnipotent Daddy Warbucks. After Gray's death in 1968, "Little Orphan Annie" was unsuccessfully continued by other hands until the editors decided to go into reprints of the old Gray stories in 1974. © Chicago Tribune–New York News Syndicate.

Little Annie Rooney, Brandon Walsh and Darrell McClure. Unlike Gray's spunky little heroine, this Annie (who ran in the papers from 1929 to 1966) was closer to the tear-jerking tradition of Little Nell and countless other orphan girls of the novels, stage and screen. She also displayed a definite, if seemingly innocent, sexuality. © King Features Syndicate.

Ma Feitelbaum, Milt Gross ("Nize Baby"). Mrs. Feitelbaum was the stereotype of the Jewish mother in this very funny chronicle of a lower-class New York family. A genuinely warm and rip-roaringly funny strip, "Nize Baby" only ran from 1926 to 1929, in spite of its popularity with readers. © New York World.

Vanilla, Harry Hershfield and Darrell McClure ("Vanilla and the Villains"). Ghost-written by the irrepressible Harry Hershfield, the continuity of "Vanilla" ran true to the earlier model of "Desperate Desmond." Vanilla Graingerfield was a heroine of truly epic disposition, as she thwarted the designs of evil-looking and sinister-named villains, with the help of her boyfriend Stonewall, and ran an unending gauntlet of hair-raising ordeals. The strip ran from 1928 to the end of 1929.

Etta Kett, Paul Robinson. Created in 1925, Etta Kett has shown herself as a paragon of modesty and good manners (as befits her name) for half a century. A vivacious, outgoing, dark-haired young lady with impeccable taste in clothes and fashions, her existence has been one long and proper whirlwind of dates and parties. It has also been one long yawn for the readers. © King Features Syndicate.

Toots, Jimmy Murphy ("Toots and Casper"). While started in July 1919, "Toots and Casper" only hit its stride in the 1920's. Toots (who, like her husband, never had a surname, a not unusual conceit of comic strips of the time) was an engaging and loving young wife whose domestic conflicts were confined to good-humored differences over Toots's daring clothes, or Casper's ogling of the good-looking babysitters hired to watch the couple's infant, Buttercup. "Toots and Casper" was discontinued in 1956.

Fritzi Ritz, Ernie Bushmiller. Bushmiller drew "Fritzi Ritz," starting in 1925. Fritzi was a dark, curly-haired doll, much in the mold of countless other comic strip girls of the time. What she had going for her was a good sense of humor (a quality promiscuously absent from most of her cartoon rivals). Fritzi's alarums and contretemps (often caused by her inept boyfriend, Phil Fumble) were reasonably funny. When Bushmiller introduced Fritzi's niece, Nancy, to the strip, however, the leading lady was soon upstaged by the antics of the newcomer. In the 1940's the feature was rechristened "Nancy," and Aunt Fritzi only appears in it as a supporting character.

Petting Patty, Jefferson Machamer. Petting Patty was one more entry in the pretty girl sweepstakes, a field that was becoming more and more crowded as the 1920's drew to a close. Patty, who made her debut in the middle of the decade, found her dreams of being "petted" often frustrated by reluctant males. Jefferson left the strip in the 1930's to start a weekly gag panel on the same theme, "Gags and Gals," which met with greater success than "Patty." © King Features Syndicate.

Cylinda Oyl, E.C. Segar ("Thimble Theater"). Cylinda was the very transient wife of Olive's brother, Castor. Looking all the more glamorous in comparison to the homely Olive, Cylinda did not tarry long in the company of ne'er-do-well Castor, and soon left for more promising horizons. Her presence in the "Thimble Theater" of the 1920's was a welcome change from the usual sloppy crew of characters that populated the strip. © King Features Syndicate.

Phyllis Blossom, Frank King ("Gasoline Alley"). Love came into the gentle world of Gasoline Alley when the dyed-in-the-wool bachelor Walt Wallet started courting the tender, understanding Phyllis Blossom in the mid-1920's. The romance was crowned by their wedding in 1926. Unlike so many comic strip wives Phyllis did not turn into a nagging, frustrated housewife. Her qualities of tolerance and wisdom only blossomed (no pun intended) further, and she proved a great help to her more impulsive husband, saving him from many a dishonest scheme. "Gasoline Alley," which started in 1918, has been continued, following the creator's death in 1969, by Bill Perry and Dick Moores. © Chicago Tribune-New York News Syndicate.

Little Egypt, Frank Willard ("Moon Mullins"). Little Egypt was the lovelight of the rather disreputable Moon. A dancer in a carnival show (not unlike her namesake, the real-life Little Egypt of scandalous fame) the high-spirited hoofer proved more than a match for Moon's underhanded ardors. (Begun in 1923, "Moon Mullins" is now done by Ferd Johnson, who succeeded Willard, following the latter's death in 1958.) © Chicago Tribune-New York News Syndicate.

Pearl, Rube Goldberg ("Boob McNutt"). "Boob McNutt" had been only an indifferently successful strip when, in 1922, Goldberg decided to have his simpleton hero fall for a flapper named Pearl. The adventures that followed (in which Boob foiled the murderous attemps of his rivals, aided and abetted by Pearl's father, Toby) soon won over the public. Pearl herself was a rather innocuous figure, only enlightened by her unswerving devotion to her boobish boyfriend. "Boob McNutt" ran from 1915 to 1934. © Rube Goldberg.

Tango, Roy Crane ("Wash Tubbs"). In the course of his innumerable wanderings, Wash Tubbs, Roy Crane's diminutive hero, had met countless beauties (usually double his size) with whom he would invariably fall in love. None of them, however, matched the fiery Tango, the tiger tamer, who would not hesitate to use the whip on her bemused boyfriend. © NEA Service.

The Countess, Roy Crane ("Wash Tubbs"). Another of the shady ladies that Wash Tubbs was always falling for, ever since he had started on the road in 1924, the Countess was a clever con woman who tried to cheat Wash out of his reward money. She had him convicted of her partner's murder, dispossessed of all his money, and ruined in the eyes of his friends, before meeting her come-uppance in the end. © NEA Service.

Beautiful Bab, Murat "Chic" Young. Beautiful Bab was only the second in a long line of female characters created by the prolific pen of Chic Young. Bab was a resourceful and quite emancipated college-girl whose pranks on and off campus often got her into trouble. She lasted but a few years—from 1922 to 1924. © Bell Syndicate.

The Kid Sister, Lyman Young. Lyman Young followed in his younger brother Chic's footsteps when he created "The Kid Sister" in 1927. The strip was an early prefiguration of "Juliet Jones," with its two sisters, the older, dark-haired Trixie Dale, and the younger, blonde Jane (the heroine of the title). The plots were pure soap-opera, full of scheming rivals and handsome suitors. The feature came to an end in 1935 (after having had the distinction of being ghosted by Alex Raymond for the best part of 1933). © King Features Syndicate.

Kitty McCoy, Billy DeBeck ("Barney Google"). A well-established convention of the comics was that the smaller the hero the bigger his retinue of lovely girls. Kitty McCoy was a haughty heiress only interested in Barney's lucky streak at the racetrack. ("Barney Google" started in 1919, but hit its stride in the following decade and is still in existence today, drawn by Fred Lasswell.) © King Features Syndicate.

Betty Lou Barnes, Hal Forrest and Glen Chaffin ("Tailspin Tommy"). Described by the authors as possessing "more nerve than most men," Betty Lou was a daredevil aviatrix and the founder (along with her two male companions, the handsome Tailspin Tommy and the comical Skeeter) of a shaky airline company named Three-Point Airlines. The spunky brunette faced innumerable perils and dangers in adventures which carried her to the far corners of the earth, from the equatorial forests of the Amazon to the icy wastes of Alaska. "Tailspin Tommy" pursued its adventurous career from 1928 to the early 1940's. © Bell Syndicate.

Peggy Mills, Richard Calkins ("Skyroads"). Peggy was also an indomitable lady-pilot who braved the elements and every peril that man and nature could conjure in her conquest of new horizons. With such heroines as Betty Lou and Peggy, we are already leaving the prevalent mood of the frivolous Twenties, and stand on the threshold of the more venturesome Thirties. ("Skyroads," was created by Dick Calkins in 1929, at the same time as his better-known feature, "Buck Rogers.") © National Newspaper Syndicate.

Belinda Blinks, Charles William Kahles ("Hairbreadth Harry"). © Jessie Kahles Straut.

Mary-Jane, Richard Felton Outcault ("Buster Brown").

Mary-Jane, Richard Felton Outcault ("Buster Brown").

Bécassine, Caumery (Maurice Languereau) and J. P. Pinchon. © Gauthier-Languereau.

Miss Peachtree, Ed Carey ("Simon Simple").

Lulu, F. M. Howarth ("Lulu and Leander").

Lady Bountiful, Gene Carr ("Lady Bountiful").

Dixie Dugan, John Striebel and J. P. McEvoy. © McNaught Syndicate.

Fritzi Ritz, Ernie Bushmiller. © United Feature Syndicate.

Jane Arden, Jack McGuire. © Register and Tribune Syndicate.

Sally, Jack Callahan ("Freddie the Sheik"). © King Features Syndicate.

Toots, Jimmy Murphy ("Toots and Casper"). © King Features Syndicate.

Rosie, George McManus ("Rosie's Beau"). © King Features Syndicate.

Tillie the Toiler, Russ Westover. © King Features Syndicate.

The Stenog, A. E. Hayward ("Somebody's Stenog"). © Ledger Syndicate.

Flapper Fanny, Gladys Parker. © NEA Service.

Mamma Katzenjammer, Rudolph Dirks ("The Katzenjammer Kids"). © King Features Syndicate.

Connie, Frank Godwin. © Ledger Syndicate.

Mrs. Newlywed, George McManus ("The Newlyweds and Their Baby").

Fluffy Ruffles, Wallace Morgan.

Hildegard Hamhocker, T. K. Ryan ("Tumbleweeds").

Phyllis, Gene Carr.

Jennie Dare, Russell Keaton ("Flyin' Jenny").
© Bell Syndicate.

Minnie Ha-Cha, Allen Saunders and Elmer Woggon ("Big Chief Wahoo"). © Field Newspaper Syndicate.

Betty Boop, Bud Counihan. © King Features Syndicate.

The Flame, Will Gould ("Red Barry"). © King Features Syndicate.

THE ROYAL ROAD TO ADVENTURE 1930-1939

The 1930's was the decade of adventure: the theme was universal. It was at the heart of the novels of Hemingway and Malraux, and occupied the central thoughts of Saint-Exupéry and Graham Greene. On the screen the heroic theme was sounded time and again in the films of John Ford, Howard Hawks and William Wellman. Crushed by the Depression, powerless to check the ominous drift towards a second world war, never did man so desperately need a dream in which he was again master of his fate.

The comics followed (and in some cases preceded) this general trend; freeing themselves from their humorous origins they were to find the royal road to adventure. (Some of the early self-styled critics of the medium could not comprehend this transformation; "the funnies aren't funny anymore," they bemoaned in unison, as though the comic strip was some archaic form, as fixed and unchanging as Egyptian bas-reliefs.) No longer a comic figure or a familiar type, the protagonist of the adventure strip was the direct descendant of the epic hero, the knight errant, the vagabond prince, all the archetypes of mythology and folklore. In his modern guise he becomes the adventurer, roaming the world, oblivious of the conventions of straight society, and contemptuous of middle-class pieties, only intent upon the object of his quest.

In the adventure strip women first appeared as the girl friend or companion of the hero. Buck Rogers had Wilma Deering; Dick Tracy, Tess Trueheart; and the Phantom, Diana Palmer. The relationships between men and women in these new, uncharted territories became perforce more ambiguous and much more sex-laden. Whether to counterpoint or complement the increasingly violent action, eroticism came to flower and fruition, as an essential component of the story-line. Girls were depicted with increasing lasciviousness as ingenious plot devices allowed for their representation in strongly suggestive poses: clothes torn from a quivering body, faces erotically convulsed in terror, intimate and furtive gestures dictated by the presence of danger, etc. Noel Sickles and Frank Robbins included bevies of bad girls and beauties in distress in **Scorchy Smith**; Clarence Gray ushered in a long parade of half-clad princesses, seductive temptresses and alluring female warriors in **Brick Bradford**; even Ralph Fuller delighted in picturing every possible kind of buxom maiden in his medieval mock-epic, **Oaky Doaks.**

Alex Raymond was especially adept at mixing the games of love with those of violence. Dale Arden, Flash Gordon's love interest, saw her virtue, as well as her person, in constant danger. She was often depicted on the verge of being raped, tortured, whipped or otherwise victimized by jealousy-crazed rivals, or cruelly tormented by sadistic jail-keepers: she could have easily passed for a younger sister of Sade's ill-starred Justine. On the other hand, Burne Hogarth's heroines were made of quite a different mettle. The fierce amazon warriors and intrepid female explorers of **Tarzan** displayed a strength of character not far below that of the lord of the jungle.

Soon these female leads tired of their almost exclusively decorative roles and started stepping out of the "damsel in distress" stereotype. Dale Arden saved Flash Gordon's life on several occasions, and she once fought tooth-and-nail against an assassin sent by Flash's arch-foe, Ming the Merciless, to murder the hero. If Diana Palmer, the Phantom's elusive fiancée, has often been used as a lure to draw the masked avenger into some sinister trap, she has also helped him get out of situations in which her feminine guile proved more effective than his masculine brawn. Wilma, of course, showed herself to be as resourceful and daring as Buck Rogers, and her frequent temperamental outbursts left little doubt that here was one girl over whom no male could lord. Even Tess Trueheart, passive and resigned as she often was, found occasions for convincing her too smug detective boyfriend that she could not be taken for granted.

From the mid-1930's on, this mood of feminine assertiveness was all but universal in the funny papers. Betty Lou could hold her own with Tailspin Tommy; Molly Day, the red-headed undercover cop, could prove as strong and cunning as her companions in **Radio Patrol**; and Mississippi, the tough-talking, golden-hearted newspaper gal, was more than a match for any of the shady characters striding across the **Red Barry** strip. Even the more traditionally portrayed heroines, such as Gina Lane (**Charlie Chan**), Mercedes Colby (**Don Winslow**), and Becky Groggins (**Abbie n' Slats**), came into their own as the 1930's were drawing to a close.

Lois Lane, the female lead of **Superman**, is a special case among comic strip heroines. She is, as every red-blooded American under the age of 50 knows, hopelessly in love with the Man of Steel, while at the same time haughtily spurning the sheepish advances of Superman's alter ego, Clark Kent. The Freudian implications of this weird **ménage-à-trois** were never fully realized by the authors, but this story device projects a neurotic parable reflective of our disturbed times. While Superman was deemed too good for any woman, no woman would consider Clark good enough for her. Thus, in both of his impersonations (as super-hero and as super-schlemiel), Superman-Clark Kent could find no sexual fulfillment (and neither could Lois).

A few girls did, however, achieve equal star status and became full-fledged heroines in their own right, with a feature named after them. The most accomplished of these was without a doubt Connie, whose full name, Constance Kurridge, was a suitable shorthand for the many qualities she displayed all through the 1930's (and well into the 1940's), once Godwin had allowed her to eschew her society-girl role. She excelled as a private eye, a newspaper reporter, even as a military strategist, and, above all, as an interplanetary explorer who could disarm alien creatures with the same cool aplomb that she displayed with men of this earth. Her exploits, which showed her capable of doing anything a man could do, mark her as the ultimate pioneer of woman's liberation in the funny papers.

A few other heroines followed in Connie's footsteps. **Myra North** was a blatant, if pleasant, imitation displaying the same cool, blonde attractiveness as Connie. Jenny Dare (heroine of Russell Keaton's **Flyin' Jenny**) was more spirited and wisecracking, as she went into the wild blue yonder, to beat her male competitors in air race after harrowing air race. And, finally, there was **Sheena, Queen of the Jungle,** the most flamboyant of all paper heroines, and a worthy answer to Tarzan of the Apes.

The many sultry villainesses who populated the adventure strips of the 1930's illustrated even more of a reaction against the sweet feminine roles assigned to women by male syndicate editors. Ardala Valmar, Killer Kane's fiery bombshell of a mate in **Buck Rogers**, was just as devious, scheming and underhanded as her accomplice, and proved as much of a foe to Buck as the sinister Killer. Sala, having been spurned by the Phantom, turned into the masked avenger's most implacable enemy, and the Flame, an Eurasian version of the **femme fatale**, showed herself as a deadly adversary for Red Barry.

From this promising seedbed of rebellion a new stereotype soon emerged: that of the reformed bad girl (a convention of many Hollywood movies of the time, not coincidentally). Princess Aura, Ming's headstrong daughter, was best in her role as arch-rival of Dale Arden for Flash Gordon's affections, but later married and turned into a model wife, much to the readers' loss; and **Prince Valiant** fans may remember that Aleta, Queen of the Misty Isles, had once lured Valiant's companions into a deadly ambush, before she was finally subjugated by the black-haired knight. In the same vein Lil' de Vrille had been a smuggler and outlaw who was won over to Jungle Jim's cause only after being outwitted (and overwhelmed) by the handsome animal hunter; and Princess Narda had tried to do Mandrake in on several occasions, before settling into an apparently morganatic union of sorts with the magician.

One comic strip author who has won just fame for his memorable portayal of female characters is Milton Caniff who, in **Terry and the Pirates**, created an unparalleled gallery of beautiful girls. Of all the seductive women in the strip three especially stand out: Normandie Sandhurst (**née** Drake), Burma, and the Dragon-Lady. Chronologically, the Dragon-Lady came first: she was conceived at the outset of the feature, as an Eurasian villainess, the leader of a band of cutthroats and murderers, whose real name was Lai Choi San (allegedly meaning "Mountain of Wealth" in Chinese). Enigmatic yet devastating, with high cheekbones and jet-black hair, the Dragon-Lady was also intelligent and highly sophisticated, well-versed in the ways of the world (and of men), conversant in Confucius and Shakespeare, and without illusion. Next came Normandie, spoiled, capricious and headstrong, who would marry the boorish Tony Sandhurst out of spite, and remain faithful to him out of duty and a sense of **noblesse oblige**. The golden-haired, golden-hearted Burma, a fugitive from justice, completes this triptych: brash, obvious and almost outrageously endowed with lascivious charms, she went after her man with single-minded determination.

The focus of the girls' attentions was Pat Ryan, Terry's adult companion, and the real hero of the strip. The handsome adventurer was forever flitting from one seductress to the next, never quite deciding, never quite surrendering. Thus, in typical fashion, the girls were seen through a man's eye: flawed in the individual, but perfect in the aggregate, they represented the wish-fullfilment of every man's fantasy; while the contradictions of man's sexual and affective desires were reflected in their symbolic trinity of opposites: the senses (Burma), the head (Dragon-Lady), and the heart (Normandie).

Some cases however seem to defy classification. Olive Oyl in the 1930's finally found her mate in the person of the salty, hot-tempered and invincible Popeye, the one-eyed sailor. This happy event did not appreciably improve Olive Oyl's temperament: still ungracious, surly and prissy as before, she continued to parade her gawky figure and disagreeable disposition, as a permanent affront to the sexy creatures and lovely lasses that surrounded her on the comic pages. Al Capp's Daisy Mae had a charm and figure worthy of any among the comic strip heroines, but a brain that was fixated on the loutish Li'l Abner, and a single-minded aim, that of bringing her reluctant boyfriend to the altar, by means fair or foul. On the other side of the Atlantic, a young English lady named Jane, (in a strip of that title by Norman Pett), was displaying an alarming propensity for shedding her clothes on the most embarassing occasions, a harbinger of generations of comic strip heroines to come.

The traditions of the preceding decade were also dying hard. John Held, the most prolific chronicler of the Jazz Age and its idiosyncrasies, came up with **Merely Margy**, a definite throwback to the era of flappers, bathtub gin and raccoon coats, peopled with the angular ladies so fashionable in earlier times. Chic Young had the same idea with Blondie, a scatterbrained gold digger out of place in the impoverished circumstances of the 1930's; more adaptable than Held, however, he had the sense to marry off his heroine and eventually transform her into a model of domestic virtue. This timely metamorphosis made **Blondie** the most widely read comic feature of this and several succeeding decades.

In the 1930's comic strip heroines (or at least a number of them) enjoyed popular recognition equal to that of any male protagonist of the funnies. Even the eight-pagers, the pornographic comic books that could be bought under any drugstore counter, paid them the (back-handed) honor of starring them in their pages: thus Tillie the Toiler, Winnie Winkle and Blondie were depicted in situations and positions that could not be seen in the comic papers.

Wilma Deering, Phil Nowlan and Dick Calkins ("Buck Rogers"). Started in 1929, "Buck Rogers" can be said to have been (along with "Tarzan") the herald of the new age of adventure in the comics. Wilma was the girlfriend and plucky associate of the hero, Buck Rogers, an American pilot of WW I who found himself stranded in 25th-century America, overrun by Mongol invaders. Wilma proved herself a resourceful, courageous and headstrong heroine, and a far cry from her more sedate sisters of the 1920's. "Buck Rogers" itself met with instant success and lasted until 1967. © National Newspaper Syndicate.

Tess Truehart, Chester Gould ("Dick Tracy"). The sweetheart (and later wife) of Gould's strong-jawed detective hero, Tess was a moody and unpredictable lady, often involved in predicaments of her own creation. Her marriage (in 1949) took her off center stage. © Chicago Tribune-Daily News Syndicate.

Dale Arden, Alex Raymond ("Flash Gordon"). Dale Arden went along with Flash Gordon (and Professor Zarkov) on the fateful rocket flight to the alien planet Mongo. Since then she has known countless adventures and perils, often pretexts for her blond boyfriend hero to rescue her from the clutches of despicable ruffians whose libidinous intents were all too apparent. "Flash Gordon" has known a brilliant and eventful career since its creation by Alex Raymond in 1934. It is now being done by Dan Barry, brother of Sy Barry. © King Features Syndicate.

Diana Palmer, Lee Falk and Ray Moore ("The Phantom"). The Phantom's elusive fiancée, Diana was also a heroine in her own right, capable of standing up to many a male opponent. She used guile, however, in preference to muscle in her dealings with pirates, kidnappers and other assorted miscreants. "The Phantom," started in 1936, is still running (Sy Barry is currently drawing the feature).

Molly Day, Charles Schmidt and Eddie Sullivan ("Radio Patrol"). Molly was a tough, no-nonsense undercover detective who brooked no sarcasm from the rugged police sergeant, the red-headed Pat, with whom she was secretly in love. Molly's first love, however, was her job, and she displayed an impressive combination of pluck, stamina, determination and cleverness in her unceasing efforts to nab racketeers, extortionists and gang leaders. Started in 1933 (as "Pinkerton Jr."), "Radio Patrol" ran until 1950.

Mississippi, Will Gould ("Red Barry"). Another representative of the new school of professionally-dedicated women, Mississippi (her surname was never given) was a tough, resourceful news reporter whose eagerness for a scoop often landed her in all kinds of trouble with both malefactors and her detective boyfriend, square-chinned Red Barry. The feature itself was deemed too violent by syndicate editors and had only a short run (from 1934 to 1939). © King Features Syndicate.

Gina Lane, Al Andriola ("Charlie Chan"). Gina Lane provided the feminine relief in the "Charlie Chan" newspaper strip (1938–42). The fiancée of Chan's handsome assistant, Kirk Barrow, Gina was an actress, but her love of both adventure and Kirk involved her in most of the Chinese detective's cases.

Becky Groggins, Rae Van Buren ("Abbie n' Slats") The daughter of the shiftless, smelly "Bathless Groggins," Becky was the girlfriend of Slats Scrapple (the titular hero) and a decidedly handsome and determined young lady. Her dark good looks appreciably brightened the pages of "Abbie n' Slats" from the feature's inception in 1937 to its demise in 1971. (The strip had the further distinction of having been created by Al Capp.)

Sybil, Hal Foster ("Tarzan"). In the comic strips, Tarzan's mate Jane was rarely seen. In her absence the apeman often fell prey to the advances of exotic princesses and determined adventuresses. Sybil was a white explorer who held sway over a tribe of cowering natives; her unruly passion for Tarzan proved her undoing. Foster was the first illustrator of the comic strip version of "Tarzan," which started in 1929. © ERB, Inc.

Princess Leecia, Burne Hogarth ("Tarzan"). Another attractive lady who was to cross the apeman's path, Princess Leecia saved Tarzan's life on their very first encounter. The lord of the jungle repaid her in kind by snatching her from the clutches of the brutish tyrant to whom she was betrothed, the unsavory Jagurt. Burne Hogarth had taken over the "Tarzan" Sunday page from Hal Foster in 1937, and had brought it to unparalleled heights of acclaim before definitively abandoning it in 1950. The feature is now being drawn by Russ Manning. © ERB, Inc.

Mickey, Noel Sickles ("Scorchy Smith"). John Terry had originated "Scorchy Smith" in 1930, but Noel Sickles (who had taken over in 1934) was the artist most responsible for its fame. Sickles was, like his friend Caniff, noted for his illustrated women. Mickey was a venturesome and determined young girl, not unlike some of the screen characters played by Jean Arthur, to whom she bore more than passing resemblance. © AP Newsfeatures.

Zora, Frank Robbins ("Scorchy Smith"). After Sickles had left the strip (in 1936), "Scorchy Smith" passed into the hands of Bert Christman, then to Howell Dodd. Frank Robbins took over in 1939 and proved to be Sickles's worthy continuator. Zora had originally been a spy intent on wrecking Scorchy's secret mission, but she was later won over to the right side, thanks to the hero's irresistible charm. "Scorchy Smith" folded in 1961. © AP Newsfeatures.

June Salisbury, William Ritt and Clarence Gray ("Brick Bradford"). The daughter of scientist Van Atta Salisbury, and Brick's most constant girlfriend, June was featured only in the daily version of "Brick Bradford." Her role was mainly decorative, although she did, on occasion, display some qualities of courage and resourcefulness. The "Brick Bradford" daily strip was originated in 1933; in 1952 Clarence Gray relinquished the drawing of the strip to Paul Norris who is still doing it today. © King Features Syndicate.

Rota, William Ritt and Clarence Gray ("Brick Bradford"). Among the beauties always surrounding Brick in the Sunday page, the fiery, red-headed Rota was one of the most spectacular. She was an iron-willed dictator who ruled her subjects with an implacable hand in an exotic civilization of the year 1,001,942 A.D. She finally succumbed, however, to the virile charm and superior cunning of the hero. The weekly page of "Brick Bradford" started in 1934. Paul Norris is currently drawing the feature, along with the daily version. © King Features Syndicate.

Lois Lane, Jerome Siegel and Joe Shuster ("Superman"). Lois Lane has been in love with Superman from the very first time that the adventures of the "Man of Tomorrow" reached the newsstands. The triangle formed by Lois, Superman and Clark Kent (Superman's meek reporter alter ego) must be one of the more celebrated affairs in popular history. In some of the "imaginary stories" Lois actually discovered that Clark was Superman and even got him to marry her (as in this example); this would invariably turn out to have been a dream, however. First sprung on an unsuspecting populace in June 1938, Superman is still going strong, carried on by a multitude of artists and writers. © DC Comics Inc.

Connie, Frank Godwin. In the 1930's Connie really took flight. No longer the society girl of her early adventures, she went to work first as a reporter, then as a private eye. Her adventures took her as far as Mexico and South America, and even to Soviet Russia. She triumphed foremost in the field of interplanetary exploration, discovering unknown civilizations on Mars, Jupiter, Venus and other planets of the solar system. © Ledger Syndicate.

Jenny Dare, Russell Keaton ("Flyin' Jenny"). Jenny Dare was the first aviatrix to have her own comic strip. Not only could she stand up to any rival male pilot in pylon contests or air races, but she was a lot better looking, too. "Flyin' Jenny" originated in 1939 and was unfortunately discontinued in 1946, following the untimely death of its creator, Russell Keaton. © Bell Syndicate.

Myra North, Charles Coll. Myra was a "special nurse" whose love of adventure and mystery took her very far afield from the nursing profession. She traveled to the mythical country of Morentia "torn by civil war," saved a crowned head or two, and fought the evil designs of sinister villains such as Hyster and Professor Zero. Her boyfriend was named Jack Lane. (It may—or may not—be significant that so many of the comics' subsidiary characters are named Lane. There is Lois Lane, Gina Lane, Jack Lane—not to mention Margo Lane of "The Shadow" in pulp magazines.) "Myra North, Special Nurse" started in 1936 and lasted only to 1941. © NEA Service.

Ardala Valmar, Phil Nowlan and Dick Calkins ("Buck Rogers"). Ardala Valmar, the girlfriend of the fiendish Killer Kane, was Buck Rogers's most implacable female foe. Her satanic imagination often came close to proving Buck's undoing. She is perhaps the best illustration of "the female of the species is more dangerous than the male" syndrome in the comics. © National Newspaper Syndicate.

Sheena, Robert Webb. Sheena, Queen of the Jungle, was the most famous denizen of the jungle next to Tarzan. A flamboyant blonde bombshell with a full figure, she would swing from treetop to treetop in search of safaris to rescue or of malefactors to hunt down. Credited to the fictitious "W. Morgan Thomas," Sheena was actually the brainchild of comics producer S.M. "Jerry " Iger. She spun out her exploits with wild abandon from 1937 to 1953. © S.M. Iger.

Sala, Lee Falk and Ray Moore ("The Phantom"). In contrast to Ardala, Sala represents a good example of the "Hell hath no fury as a woman scorned" school of feminine psychology. Her feats of outlawry were prompted, as often as not, by her unrequited love for "the ghost-who-walks." © King Features Syndicate.

Princess Narda, Lee Falk and Phil Davis ("Mandrake"). Princess Narda, of the mythical kingdom of Cockaigne, made her appearance the very first year of the strip (1934), trying to murder Mandrake in order to protect her no-good brother Segrid. Since then she has been the magician's constant companion in danger. Phil Davis drew Narda in a nonchalant yet winsome way until his death in 1964. "Mandrake the Magician" is currently being carried on by Harold "Fred" Fredericks. © King Features Syndicate.

The Flame, Will Gould ("Red Barry"). The Flame was a Eurasian gang leader who terrorized the Chinatown of an unnamed American city. She displayed uncommon cunning and courage and was only brought to heel by Red Barry's dogged efforts. Gould's graphic style, a cross between Raymond's drybrush technique and Caniff's atmospheric impressionism, was at its best in the depiction of slinky and sexy villainesses. © King Features Syndicate.

Princess Aura, Alex Raymond ("Flash Gordon"). The fiery and headstrong daughter of Ming the Merciless, Aura became infatuated with her father's arch-enemy, Flash Gordon, as soon as she laid eyes on him. She thwarted her father's will on more than one occasion for love of the blond earthman. She later transferred her affections to Prince Barin of Arboria (whom she married) and was to become one of Flash's more trustworthy supporters. © King Features Syndicate.

Queen Fria, Alex Raymond ("Flash Gordon"). Among the ranks of the planet Mongo's reigning monarchs, few cut as lovely and regal a figure as Queen Fria of the northern kingdom of Frigia. Although enamored of the dashing Flash (as all female characters in the strip invariably were), she found the strength to overcome her feelings of spite at being spurned by Flash, subordinating her **raisons de coeur** to the more exacting calling of **raison d'état.** © King Features Syndicate.

Lil' de Vrille, Alex Raymond ("Jungle Jim"). Lil's first appearance occurred in 1935; she was then a clever extortionist known as "the Vampire Queen." After she had been subjugated by Jungle Jim's charm, she became the gentleman adventurer's girlfriend. Her qualities of character and her intelligence made her one of the most fascinating heroines of the comic pages. "Jungle Jim" began in 1934 and ended 20 years later (and 10 years after Raymond had left the feature to join the Marines). © King Features Syndicate.

Aleta, Harold Foster ("Prince Valiant"). Prince Valiant, the handsome knight of King Arthur's court, fell in love with the elusive "Queen of the Misty Isles" at his first glimpse of her youthful and blushing beauty. He then scoured the ends of the earth in his feverish quest for the princess of his dreams, finally marrying her and fathering her children. Foster abandoned the drawing of "Prince Valiant" (which he had created in 1937) to John Cullen Murphy in 1971. © King Features Syndicate.

Grace Powers, Dashiell Hammett and Alex Raymond ("Secret Agent X-9"). Celebrated novelist Dashiell Hammett and gifted artist Alex Raymond created "Secret Agent X-9" (which Bill Blackbeard called "the gala wedding of the pulps to the comics") in 1934. Among the many female characters who crossed X-9's path, none was more fascinating than Grace Powers, the scheming, cynical wife (and soon widow) of millionaire Tarleton Powers. For all her hard-bitten cynicism, Grace succumbed to X-9's sullen sexiness, and she died shielding the G-man from the fire of a gang leader's gun. Both Raymond and Hammett abandoned "Secret Agent X-9" in 1935; it is currently being carried on (as "Secret Agent Corrigan") by Al Williamson. © King Features Syndicate.

Nell, Harry O'Neill ("Broncho Bill"). Broncho Bill was the name of the teenaged leader of a gang of youthful vigilantes known as "the Rangers," and Nell was his spirited girlfriend and aide-de-camp. Their relationship was entirely innocent (this was an innocent age), and Nell often proved to be a good comrade in a tight spot. Started in 1930, "Broncho Bill" finally rode into the sunset at the end of the 1940's. © United Feature Syndicate.

The Dragon-Lady, Milton Caniff ("Terry and the Pirates"). The dreaded woman pirate made her first appearance on the Sunday page in 1934 (only weeks after the start of the feature) when she captured Terry and his adult companion Pat Ryan aboard a junk plying Chinese waters. Since that time she and Pat have maintained a tumultuous relationship based on mutual admiration and reciprocal distrust. The Dragon-Lady redeemed her shady reputation somewhat by her daring guerrilla war on the Japanese invaders; her name has now become a by-word of the American language. (The illustration reproduced here has never been published before: this nude figure of the Dragon-Lady was used by Caniff as a model for the strip—no pun intended!) Courtesy of the author.

Normandie Drake, Milton Caniff ("Terry and the Pirates"). A spoiled heiress (the type was a sample of the 1930's), Normandie entered Pat's life in 1935. Although mutually in love, they were kept apart by cruel fate and Normandie's scheming relatives.

Burma, Milton Caniff ("Terry and the Pirates"). Burma entered the scene in 1936, the last of the trinity of sexy women to tug at Pat Ryan's heartstrings. A fugitive from justice, the wisecracking Burma was the legendary bad girl with a heart of gold.

Betty Blake, Allen Dean ("King of the Royal Mounted"). Betty made her appearance in the very first episode of "King" when she and her brother Kid were rescued from the clutches of a gang of outlaws by the indomitable Mountie. Betty thereafter became King's somewhat neglected girlfriend, and she was to make a number of reappearances in the strip, never quite getting her man in the end. "King of the Royal Mounted" was created by noted Western author Zane Grey in 1935, with Allen Dean as the first illustrator. The feature disappeared in 1955.

Gale, Zack Mosley ("Smilin' Jack"). "Smilin' Jack" Martin was a pilot better noted for his amorous exploits than for his aeronautic skills. He was married countless times, and among the string of sexy girls always surrounding him, the dark-haired Gale was perhaps the most interesting. Mean and assertive, as well as an accomplished flyer in her own right, she took no lip from the smooth-talking Jack. Smilin' Jack's long career started in 1933 and came to an abrupt end in 1973.

Maura, Frank Miller ("Barney Baxter"). Maura was the girlfriend of devil-may-care pilot Barney Baxter. Tired of waiting at home for her freckle-faced fiancé to return, Maura would often join him in his far-flung adventures. Frank Miller started "Barney Baxter" in 1935 (as a local feature); the strip was discontinued in 1950, following the creator's death.

Catherine, Glen Cravath ("Ted Towers"). Catherine was the blonde and pretty assistant to Ted Towers, "animal master," as the title characterized him. As handy with gun and lariat as her companion, Catherine was always in the thick of danger in the jungles of India. "Ted Towers" was credited to Frank Buck (of "Bring 'em Back Alive" fame) and lasted from 1934 to 1939; Glen Cravath was its first illustrator.

Starlight, Garrett Price ("White Boy"). Future New Yorker cartoonist Garrett Price created "White Boy" in 1933. The hero was a young Westerner captured by a tribe of Indians. Starlight was an Indian maiden "who is sympathetic with White Boy, intercedes for him, becomes his friend and advocate," as the syndicate's press release stated. The dark-tressed, sensitive Starlight disappeared from the strip when the feature changed its character and title (to "Skull Valley") in 1935. The strip, noted for its outstanding graphic qualities, disappeared soon afterwards (in 1936). © Chicago Tribune-New York News Syndicate.

Ann Howe, Ham Fisher ("Joe Palooka"). Ann Howe was the very patrician girlfriend of plebeian prizefighter Joe Palooka. Her protracted love affair with the hard-punching Joe kept the readers as much in thrall as Joe's championship bouts. Luckier than most comic strip sweethearts, Ann married Joe in 1949, to much press fanfare. © McNaught Syndicate.

A damsel in distress from "Oaky Doaks," Ralph Fuller. Oaky Doaks was a medieval knight of unusual brawn and simple wits whose exploits, as Richard Marschall put it, often saw him "involved with the plight of a pretty maiden, a fringe benefit of knighthood and a great device for . . . adding some glamor to the strip." Buxom, brash and brassy, the damsels often turned out to cause more distress to their rescuer than to their abductors. Fuller's mock-epic ran from 1935 to 1961. © AP Newsfeatures.

Minnie Ha-Cha, Allen Saunders and Elmer Woggon ("Big Chief Wahoo"). In 1936 writer Allen Saunders and artist Elmer Woggon produced the comic strip saga of a medicine man patterned after W.C. Fields and called The Great Gusto. Wahoo was his shill, and Minnie Ha-Cha his girlfriend. A onetime night club singer, Minnie was something of a flirt, and she would often throw the chief into fits of jealous rage, always falling for some handsome muscleman. © Field Newspaper Syndicate.

Oola, V.T. Hamlin ("Alley Oop"). A latter-day embodiment of Mack Sennett's bathing beauties, the pert and vivacious Oola offered a welcome contrast to her oafish (but kind-hearted) boyfriend Alley Oop. Scantily clad in a beguiling animal-skin she was every man's dream of a cave girl. Hamlin originated "Alley Oop" in 1933; the strip is now in the hands of Dave Graue. © NEA Service.

Daisy Mae, Al Capp ("Li'l Abner"). Probably one of the longest-suffering girlfriends of the comics, hillbilly maiden Daisy Mae Scraggs spent the best part of her time vainly chasing the loutish Li'l Abner Yokum, during Sadie Hawkins Day and on every other day of the year. An ironic twist of fate finally enabled her to wed the hapless Abner in a 1952 ceremony trumpeted on the covers of every magazine in the land. This crowned a courtship started in 1934, when "Li'l Abner" first appeared. © United Feature Syndicate.

Betty Boop, Bud Counihan. Betty Boop first appeared in animated films in 1930, and was transplanted to the comic strip medium in 1934. She was a tiny but resolutely feminine vamp, with a figure modeled after Mae West's. Her flirty and suggestive ways brought attacks from outraged bluenoses, which caused producer Max Fleischer to discontinue the "Betty Boop" animated cartoons in 1939 (one year after the demise of the syndicated strip).

Olive Oyl, E.C. Segar ("Thimble Theater"). In the 1930's Olive finally found a worthy mate in the person of the invincible, one-eyed Popeye the Sailor, who won the gawky spinster in a fair fight at the end of which he had decisively knocked his luckless rival, Ham Gravy, out of the running. Popeye and his "sweet pattootie" (as he was fond of calling his ungracious girlfriend) were to know many an adventure together . . . "Thimble Theater" is still in existence, 39 years after its creator's death. © King Features Syndicate.

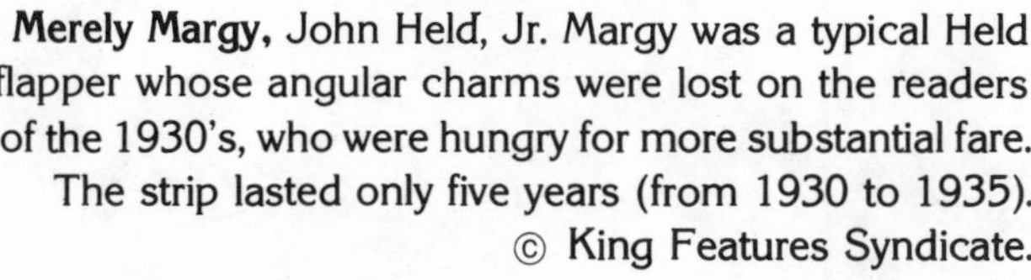
Merely Margy, John Held, Jr. Margy was a typical Held flapper whose angular charms were lost on the readers of the 1930's, who were hungry for more substantial fare. The strip lasted only five years (from 1930 to 1935). © King Features Syndicate.

Jane, Norman Pett. "Always a girl to show a leg," as British comics historian Dennis Gifford characterized her, Jane made her debut in 1932. Her very un-British (for the times) propensity for shedding her clothes earned her instant success. During WW II she turned her talents to entertaining the troops, thereby raising the morale of lonely Tommies simply by her appearance. "Jane" was finally discontinued in 1959, much to the chagrin of every red-blooded British male. (A sequel, "Jane, Daughter of Jane," was unsuccessfully tried in 1961.)

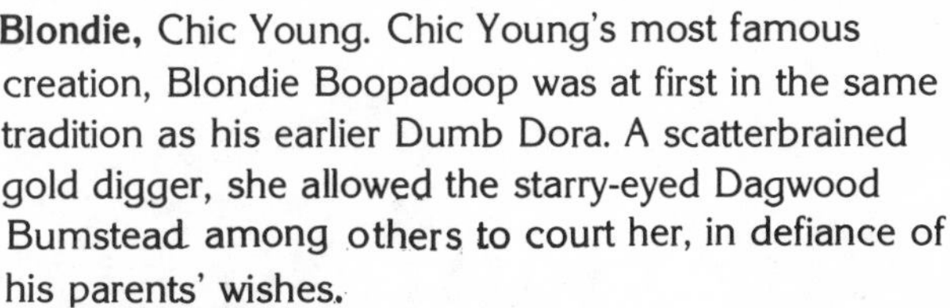

Blondie, Chic Young. Chic Young's most famous creation, Blondie Boopadoop was at first in the same tradition as his earlier Dumb Dora. A scatterbrained gold digger, she allowed the starry-eyed Dagwood Bumstead among others to court her, in defiance of his parents' wishes.

The contretemps and misadventures caused by this basic situation formed the slight canvas of the strip during its first three years, from 1930 to 1933, before the feature underwent a radical change in direction (detailed in a later chapter). © King Features Syndicate.

Tillie the Toiler. By the late 1930's comic heroines were as well-known as movie stars. The anonymous artists of the pornographic "eight-pagers" could not resist depicting the maidens of the funny pages in the most compromising situations. Here Tillie the Toiler is shown shedding all her inhibitions; but the same treatment also applied to Winnie Winkle, Blondie, and many others . . .

THE FIGHTING FORTIES 1940-1949

5

In the 1940's the comics went to war. The cartoonists did not even wait for the official declaration of belligerency, following the Pearl Harbor surprise attack of December 7, 1941, some of them having correctly identified the enemy as early as 1937. Comic strip heroes enthusiastically joined in the fight against Germans and Japanese in the most remote theaters of war. Jungle Jim was busily engaged in checking the Japanese advance in Burma; Captain Easy was foiling enemy intrigues all around the world; and Scorchy Smith fought next to the Russians on the eastern front; while Dick Tracy, X-9 and Charlie Chan battled spies and saboteurs on the home front. Tarzan obliterated a Nazi commando trying to gain a foothold in Africa, and Superman joyously demolished the Atlantic Wall; Terry grew up and joined the U.S. Air Force in the Orient; and Joe Palooka enlisted in the Army. Women became an active part of the war activities in the comics, on both sides of the conflict, whether they were alluring spies, dedicated nurses, or sultry camp-followers.

A number of comic strip heroines were not content with merely playing a secondary role in the war, but plunged into the conflict with unbridled enthusiasm. The most coruscating of these was without a doubt Wonder Woman, daughter of Hippolyte, Queen of the Amazons, who had come especially from Paradise Island to help America win the war. The Superman triangle was duplicated, only in reverse: as Wonder Woman, the heroine had only disdain for poor dull-witted Major Steve Trevor whom she had invariably to rescue from Nazi or fifth-columnist traps; under the guise of Diana Prince (which she assumed in her off-duty hours) she was hopelessly in love with the self-same Trevor who spurned her in his turn. In the olive-drab environment of WW II America, Wonder Woman cut a dashing (and fullsome) figure in her star-spangled hot pants and yellow breastplate:

she also proved the bane of Nazi spies and foreign infiltrators whom she effortlessly overcame thanks to her super-human strength, her golden lasso and her bullet-deflecting bracelets. At last little American girls had found a model to rival the boys' Man of Steel!

Another comic book super-heroine to come out of the 1940's was Mary Marvel, alias Mary Bromfield Batson, Captain Marvel's long-lost twin sister. Just like her brother, little Mary could transform herself into a super-powered avenging angel by pronouncing the fateful formula-word "Shazam!". She lacked the flashy appearance of Wonder Woman, however, and was usually relegated to a junior role in the Marvel trinity (which also included Captain Marvel, Jr.). Yet, along with Wonder Woman, she helped heroines conquer the comic book medium (which heretofore had been an almost exclusively male preserve).

Wonder Woman and Mary Marvel had both been conceived by men. Miss Fury, on the other hand, was created by a woman, Tarpe Mills. If Wonder Woman can be regarded as Superman's female counterpart, Miss Fury (or Black Fury, as she was initially called) was women's answer to Batman. She had no super-powers, but her strength, determination and cleverness allowed her to overcome her enemies, who were for the most part Axis agents sent to disrupt America's war preparations. Again like Batman Miss Fury had a dual identity: she was the flirtatious, fun-loving socialite Marla Drake by day, while she donned the tight-fitting black leopard skin to which she owed her **nom-de-guerre** at night. Unlike many other heroines Miss Fury did not shrink from violent physical action but often displayed, in a continuing series of brutal encounters, evidence of her remarkable stamina and physical powers.

Powers of a very different kind were the trademark of another war heroine, Claire Voyant, who, like Aphrodite, was born of the sea, having been plucked out of a lifeboat drifting across the Atlantic Ocean. Claire had lost her memory but was given extra-sensory perception in return. She used her telepathic faculties to locate enemy submarines and thwart the machinations of Axis agents. She was a shadowy character, however, and the absence of a past was compounded by her lack of a strong personality. She behaved more like a cardboard male character in drag than a flesh-and-blood woman. At war's end she tried to reconvert into a private eye, but without the excitement of war intrigue, the **Claire Voyant** strip lapsed into humdrum plotting, and it soon disappeared.

The girl who was possibly the most popular comic strip heroine among American fighting men was not herself a combatant: she was Miss Lace, of Milton Caniff's **Male Call** fame. Her purpose was not to help defeat the Axis powers, but to bolster the morale of the G.I.'s. Miss Lace was a scantily-clad, not overly shy, brunette bombshell whose relations (quite innocent, as it turned out) with soldiers from every branch and level of the military contributed all there was of the skimpy plot. The attraction of the strip, however, lay not with the storyline, but with the heroine herself, and the loving and seductive way in which she was depicted by the artist. Years later Caniff was to recall her conception: "Miss Lace became the single central figure [of **Male Call**], both because she had one and because a pretty girl is a nice thing to look at even if she is only a paper doll. The name 'Lace' sounded feminine, it was short and easy to remember."

The end of the war marked the return to a less violent display of woman power in the comics. Alex Raymond came back from his tour of duty with the Marine Corps to create **Rip Kirby**, whose debonair detective-hero was, in the best macho tradition, up to his neck in beautiful women. The blonde, acidulous fashion-model Honey Dorian was his official girl friend, but she received plenty of competition from all the sex-hungry women who were forever throwing themselves at the pipe-smoking private eye. Among these the most conspicuous was the sultry, dark-haired Pagan Lee, a former gangster moll reformed (of course) by Rip's unfailing powers of persuasion. At any rate **Rip Kirby** was one of the most interesting comic strips for dedicated girl-watchers.

Milton Caniff went on to create **Steve Canyon** after the war and, as might be expected, his new venture was soon filled with a bevy of alluring beauties. While they were a trifle less convincing than the earlier flaming creatures that populated **Terry,** they constituted nonetheless an engaging gallery of feminine portraits, from the auburn-haired, hard-hearted Copper Calhoon, "the she-wolf of Wall Street," to the vulnerable and troubled Summer Olson (whom Steve was later to marry). The most memorable female creation remains, however, Poteet Canyon, Steve's ward, and the very model of the woman-child.

As new strips and comic book titles were turned out, new female characters made their entrance. With Betty and Veronica, the two teen-age girls (one blonde, the other brunette) forever fighting for Archie's attentions, Bob Montana renewed the earlier tradition of **Harold Teen.** In **Drago**, Burne Hogarth beautifully delineated the intense, vibrant personality of Darby O'Day, while Ray Gotto created a worthy rival to Al Capp's Daisy Mae in the person of Dinah, the buxom blonde girl friend of his half-witted baseball hero, Ozark Ike.

Comic strips about professional women continued to come out at a fairly decent clip. Bert Whitman created the forgettable **Debbie Dean, Career Girl**; but the "career girl" of the subtitle was quite a step up from the "breadwinner" and "toiler" labels that had been affixed to girl strips of an earlier era, and was evidence of the increasing respect shown to working girls by comic strip artists and editors. Debbie herself was an heiress, "who tires of the life of a debutante," decides to embark on a career in journalism, and subsequently becomes a lady-mayor. Her adventures were only half-baked and she soon disappeared from view.

Not so Brenda Starr, who had been conceived in the first year of the decade by one of the few successful woman cartoonists, Dale Messick. A tempestuous and flamboyant creature (whom Messick had originally wanted to portray as a woman bandit but was persuaded to make into a girl reporter instead), the red-headed Brenda exhibited more than her share of neuroses, in contrast to such straight heroines of an earlier era as Connie. Perpetually torn between the demands of her career and her romantic proclivities, her life proved a long litany of frustrations. In its intensity of feeling and its sense of angst, **Brenda Starr, Reporter** was probably the most representative of all girl strips to date.

Wonder Woman, William Marston and H.G. Peter. The most famous Amazon of all landed in the United States in 1941, with the single aim of helping the Allies defeat the Axis powers. Endowed with superhuman powers, the daughter of Queen Hippolyte was, as the introduction to the opening story stated: "As lovely as Aphrodite—as wise as Athena—with the speed of Mercury and the strength of Hercules—she is known only as Wonder Woman. . . ." Wonder Woman's creator was a psychologist and he infused his theories of intersexual relationships into the feature. "Wonder Woman" has known many artists over the years. The Amazon's fame has risen of late, ever since she was discovered as an early representative of the feminist movement in the comics.

Miss Fury, Tarpe Mills. Unlike her sisters, Miss Fury (or Black Fury, as she was also called) was the brainchild of a woman. She proved true to her name as she battled, in her black leopard outfit, all varieties of evildoers and villains with ferocious intensity. Miss Fury plied the comic pages from 1940 until the last years of the decade. Her passing was much mourned by all aficionados of the bizarre. © Bell Syndicate.

Mary Marvel, C.C. Beck and Jack Binder. Mary Marvel came in answer to the astounding success of the earlier Captain Marvel. Eager to cash in on a good thing, the editors gave the "Cap" a female counterpart in the person of his long-lost twin sister. The magic word "Shazam" served for both siblings; in the case of Mary, it stood for Selena's grace, Hippolyte's strength, Ariadne's skill, Zephyrus's fleetness, Aurora's beauty, and Minerva's wisdom. When she uttered the word, Mary was transformed into a superbeing equipped with magic powers. Mary Marvel came into being in 1940, and can still be seen sporadically in Shazam! Comics. © Fawcett Publications.

Claire Voyant, Jack Sparling. A casualty of WW II, Claire Voyant had lost her memory after a disaster at sea. She proved to be adept at telepathy, a skill that came in handy in her fight against foreign agents (as well as domestic criminals). The strip debuted in 1943, and was gone by the end of the decade. © PM Newspaper.

Darby O'Day, Burne Hogarth ("Drago"). Darby was the love interest of the hero in Hogarth's all-too-brief South American saga, "Drago." While she occasionally exhibited fits of hysterical jealousy at Drago's real or imagined amorous escapades, Darby was also capable of cool thinking and unwavering loyalty. "Drago" lasted but one year (1945–46.) © Burne Hogarth.

Witch Hazel, Burne Hogarth ("Miracle Jones"). Perhaps to further give the lie to those detractors who claimed that he could not draw the female figure, Hogarth created this very alluring and sexy enchantress. Witch Hazel took the meek titular hero through the mirror and on to incredible feats of daring and bravery in the short-lived "Miracle Jones" feature (1947–48). © United Feature Syndicate.

Miss Lace, Milton Caniff ("Male Call"). Miss Lace brought cheer and comfort to the bleak environment of American men at war. Her picture could be found on many an army barracks wall alongside those of Rita Hayworth and Betty Grable. In the apt words of Stephen Becker, she was "America's best-loved vivandière." Having enlisted in 1943, "Male Call" was honorably discharged, soon after war's end, in 1946. © Milton Caniff.

Honey Dorian, Alex Raymond ("Rip Kirby"). In his new comic strip "Rip Kirby," created in 1946, Alex Raymond renewed the tradition of giving his readers a bevy of pretty girls to contemplate. Honey Dorian was private eye Rip Kirby's official girlfriend, but the blonde, curvaceous fashion model met plenty of competition for the favors of the intellectual-looking criminologist.

Pagan Lee, Alex Raymond ("Rip Kirby"). None of Honey's rivals was as resolute and suggestive as the fiery, dark-haired Pagan Lee, a sultry torch singer and former gun moll. The Rip-Honey-Pagan triangle was one of the more intriguing in the comics. After Raymond's death in 1956, the strip passed to John Prentice who is still drawing it today. © King Features Syndicate.

Christy Jameson, Roy Crane ("Buz Sawyer"). Crane's "Buz Sawyer" came out in 1943 as a war strip. Christy was the hero's sweetheart, waiting patiently at home for the return of her aviator boyfriend. This wasn't easy, as Buz was continually jetting from one end of the earth to the other, even jilting Christy for other love interests along the way. Christy always kept the faith, finally landed her restless fiancé, and even mothered a child. Involved in Buz's dangerous life, Christy has also been in mortal peril more than once.
© King Features Syndicate.

Vampirella, Enrich. © Warren Publications.

Rota, William Ritt and Clarence Gray ("Brick Bradford"). © King Features Syndicate.

Molly Day, Charles Schmidt and Eddie Sullivan ("Radio Patrol"). © King Features Syndicate.

Wonder Woman, William Marston and H. G. Peter. © DC Comics Inc.

Aleta, Harold Foster ("Prince Valiant"). © King Features Syndicate.

Sheena, Robert Webb ("Sheena, Queen of the Jungle"). © S. M. Iger.

Myra North, Charles Coll. © NEA Service.

Sala, Lee Falk and Ray Moore ("The Phantom"). © King Features Syndicate.

Lil de Vrille, Alex Raymond ("Jungle Jim").

Wonder Woman, William Marston and H. G. Peter. © DC Comics Inc.

Molly, Bob Weber ("Moose"). © King Features Syndicate.

Tess Trueheart, Chester Gould ("Dick Tracy").

Mary Worth, Ken Ernst and Allen Saunders.

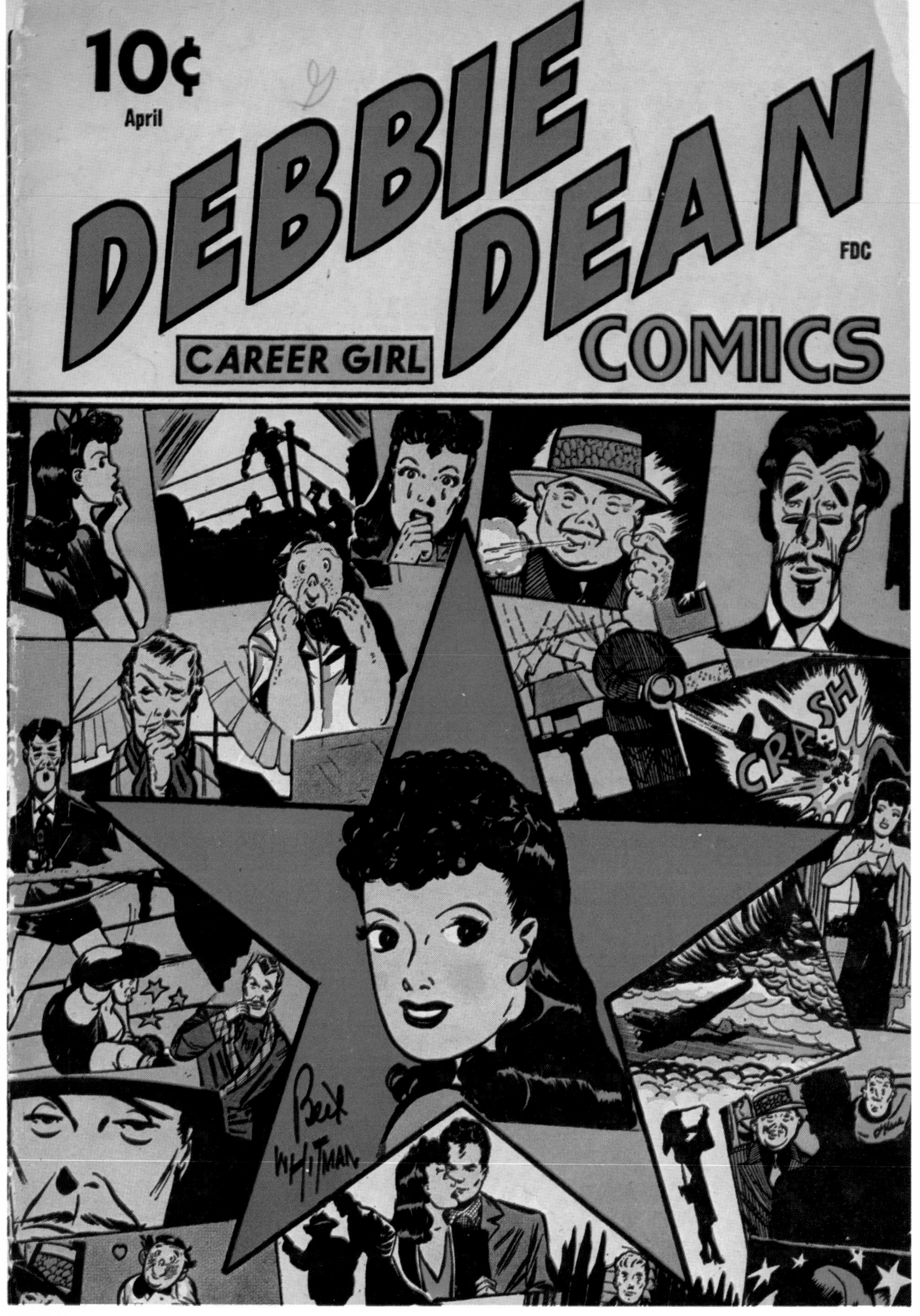

Debbie Dean, Bert Whitman. © New York Post Syndicate.

Blondie, Chic Young. © King Features Syndicate.

Miss Fury, Tarpe Mills ("Black Fury"). © Bell Syndicate.

BLACK FURY
BY Tarpé Mills

Scarlet O'Neil, Russell Stamm. © Chicago Times Syndicate.

itch Hazel, Burne Hogarth ("Miracle Jones"). © United Features Syndicate.

odelle, Guy Pellaert. © Le Terrain Vague.

Ms. Marvel, Jim Mooney and Joe Sinnott. © Marvel Comics Group.

Gwen, Stan Lee and John Romita ("Spider-Man"). © Marvel Comics Group.

Red Sonja, Frank Thorne. © Marvel Comics Group.

Stan Lee Presents: Conan the Barbarian™

The Demon out of the Deep!

THE VERDANT HILLS AND DEEP HARBORS OF ARGOS HAVE BEEN LONG LOST IN DUSK AND DISTANCE. RED SONJA... KING KULL... AYE, EVEN THE MYSTIC VISAGE OF THE DREADED THOTH-AMON... ALL HAVE ALREADY BEEN VIRTUALLY FORGOTTEN ON BOARD THE TIGRESS.

FOR, LIFE GOES ON ABOARD THIS PIRATE SHIP BOUND FOR THE BOOTY-RICH SHORES OF KUSH AND THE BLACK COAST...

SO, MY BARBARIAN-- PRACTICING YOUR ARCHERY AGAIN, I SEE?

Bêlit, Val Mayerik
(“Conan the Barbaria
© Marvel Comics Gro

Claire Voyant,
Jack Sparling.
PM Newspaper.

Gale, Zack Mosley ("Smilin' Jack"). © Chicago Tribune-New York News Syndicate.

Spider-Woman, from model sheet. © Marvel Comics Group.

Flamingo, Burne Hogarth ("Drago"). © Burne Hogarth.

Mary Perkins, Leonard Starr ("On Stage"). © Chicago Tribune-New York News Syndicate.

Princess Leecia, Burne Hogarth ("Tarzan"). © Edgar Rice Burroughs, Inc.

Isis, Mike Vosburg and Vince Colletta. © Filmation Associates.

A gallery of beauties from "Terry and the Pirates," Milton Caniff. In the 1940's Terry, now grown up, went to war (like most other heroes of the comics). His adventures weren't all martial, however, as beautiful girls kept crossing his and Pat Ryan's path. In this pageant of feminine pulchritude, special note should be given to April Kane, Terry's pert and strong-willed girlfriend. (Milton Caniff abandoned "Terry" at the end of 1946, whereupon it was taken over by George Wunder. The feature folded in 1973.) © Chicago Tribune–New York News Syndicate.

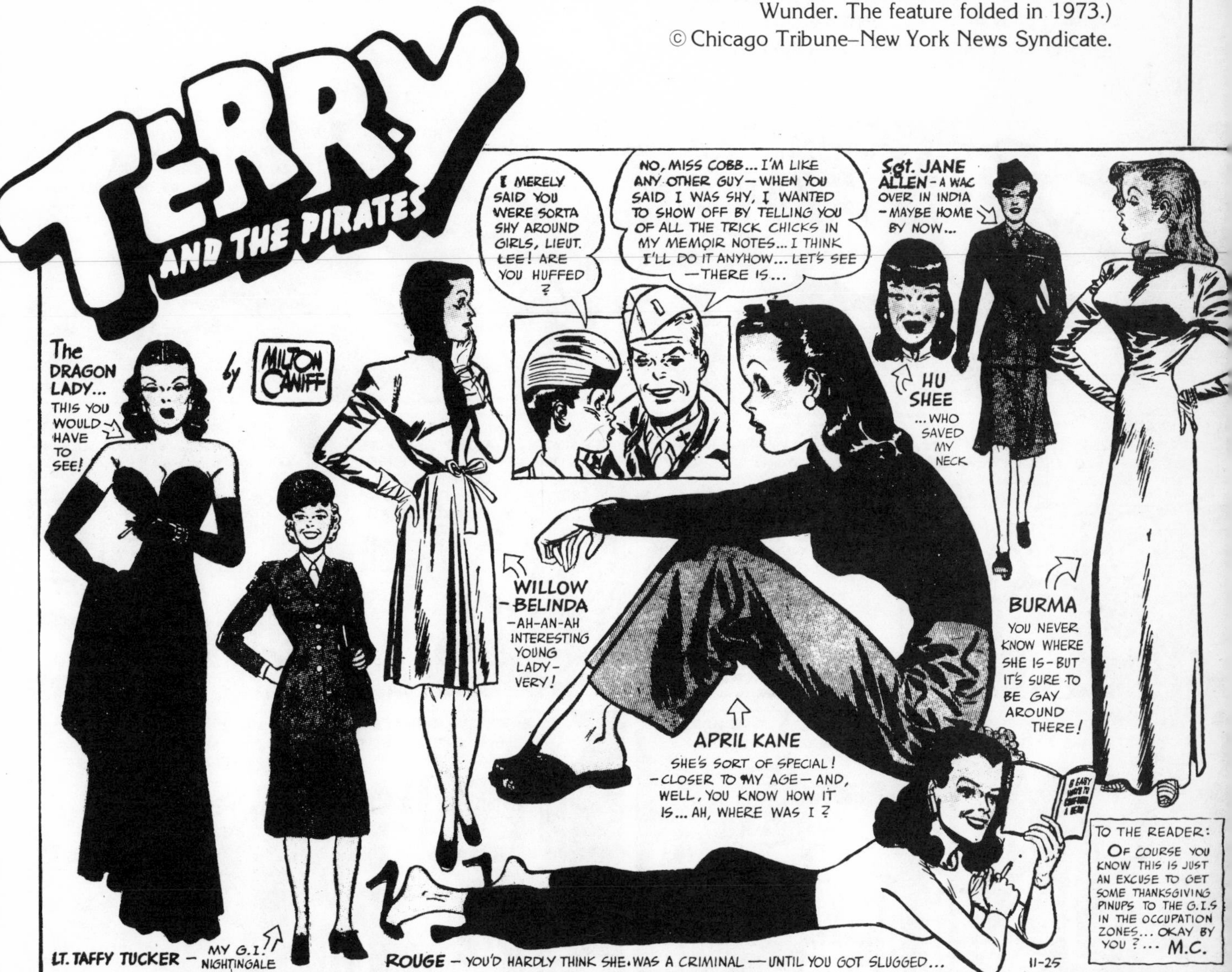

Copper Calhoon, Milton Caniff ("Steve Canyon"). Caniff did not remain idle long: in January 1947, his new strip, "Steve Canyon," made its debut. True to type it did not fail to feature an alluring gallery of villainesses, camp followers and ingénues. Copper Calhoon, a tycoon whose ruthlessness earned her the title of "she-wolf of Wall Street," went after Steve with forceful single-mindedness. © Field Newspaper Syndicate.

Summer Olson, Milton Caniff ("Steve Canyon"). Summer was Steve's true love; the pair remained locked in noble frustration over the years, however, as Summer was married to an invalid whom her sense of honor prohibited her from leaving. She later became widowed, and Steve finally could marry her in 1970. © Field Newspaper Syndicate.

Poteet Canyon, Milton Caniff ("Steve Canyon"). A latter-day entry in the **ingénue perverse** category is Poteet Canyon, Steve's niece and ward. Poteet never made a secret of the crush she had on her handsome uncle, and much hanky-panky was always suspected by the readers (a fancy tantalizingly fed by Caniff himself in his storylines). A graduate of Maumee University, and currently a working reporter, Poteet now has ample occasion to play the field, an opportunity she makes the most of. © Field Newspaper Syndicate.

Brenda Starr, Dale Messick. No more flamboyant female journalist ever strode across a newsroom than the red-haired, fierce-tempered, fickle-hearted Brenda Starr. Romance (usually doomed) dogged her footsteps, as she turned down suitor after eligible suitor in her pursuit of the secretive Basil St. John. In 1976 Dale Messick relented, however, and allowed her heroine to join Basil in wedded bliss. Started in 1940, "Brenda Starr" is still going strong.

Vesta West, Ray Bailey. "Vesta West" was an unusual Western in that it had a female protagonist, a brunette bombshell with more than her share of womanly endowments. For the rough stuff she retained the brawny Grits, her loyal male assistant; and for companionship she befriended her horse Traveller (a preference for which she could hardly have been blamed, since the animal displayed more intelligence and ingeniousness than most of the males in the strip). "Vesta West" lasted only from 1942 to 1944.
© Chicago Tribune-New York News syndicate.

Mindy, Al Andriola ("Kerry Drake"). Andriola launched his new police strip in 1943. Kerry Drake was a plainclothesman, and Mindy his long-suffering girlfriend. As was the rule in the 1950's (when the comics were being attacked for all kinds of antisocial sins) they got married, and Mindy presented a bemused Kerry with no less than quadruplets. Since then she has somewhat receded into the background (as has Kerry, who is now being overshadowed by his more flamboyant brother, Lefty).
© Field Newspaper Syndicate.

Dinah, Ray Gotto ("Ozark Ike"). Dinah was the voluptuous girlfriend and adviser to the dumb hillbilly ballplayer Ozark Ike. Were it not for his blonde adjutant (who combined the bustline of Jane Russell with the legs of Betty Grable and the hairdo of Veronica Lake), the hick hitter could not have batted .001 against the scheming shysters, crooked managers and cold-hearted gold diggers who were always throwing him curve balls. Ozark Ike started his career in 1945 and went into retirement in 1959. © King Features Syndicate.

Teena, Hilda Terry. This slight strip about the silly doings of a typical bobby-soxer was started by Hilda Terry in 1940 under the title "It's a Girl's Life!" Ms. Terry endowed her obnoxious teen-ager with more charm than meets the eye . . . © King Features Syndicate.

Chris, Warren Tufts ("Casey Ruggles"). The blonde and demure fiancee of the rugged hero of the strip, Chris often took a back seat to such flaming creatures as Lilli Lafitte, the daughter of fabled pirate Jean Lafitte, but she stuck it out with indomitable spirit in the lawless American West. "Casey Ruggles" ran from 1949 to 1954. © United Feature Syndicate.

Betty, Bob Montana ("Archie"). The fair-haired Betty was Archie Andrews's favorite girlfriend, on the turf of America's most enduring high school (it has hardly changed since the inception of the feature in 1941). She went through all the obligatory motions that were expected from a girl her age: meeting the gang after school, sipping chocolate malteds at Pop's drugstore, holding hands and exchanging sappy **mots d'amour** with her freckle-faced boyfriend, all the while fighting off the legions of schoolgirls out to steal Archie's fickle attentions. © Archie Comics.

Veronica, Bob Montana ("Archie"). The most persistent of all of Betty's rivals was without a doubt the scheming brunette Veronica Lodge for whom no trick was too underhanded in her efforts to win Archie's affections away from her schoolmate. Archie, Betty, Veronica, and the rest of the gang are still going strong, two years after their creator's death. © Archie Comics.

Pantera Bionda, Enzo Magni. Sheena's international fame gave rise to this Italian imitation. Pantera Bionda, a scantily-clad and fulsomely developed gal, lived in the jungles of Borneo and fought the Japanese in WWII. In spite of its enormous success—or, most likely, because of it—"Pantera Bionda" was forced off the newsstands under the attacks of the Catholic church after only two years (1948–1950). © SEAT.

Scarlet O'Neil, Russell Stamm. Another superwoman to spring to life in the fateful year 1940 was Scarlet O'Neil: her power was that of invisibility—she accomplished this feat simply by pressing a nerve in her left wrist, and became visible again by the same process. She fought the usual covey of wartime spies and saboteurs with creditable spirit. Scarlet disappeared for good in 1956.
© Chicago Times Syndicate.

Debbie Dean, Bert Whitman. Another girl reporter splashed across the newspaper page in 1942 (two years after Brenda Starr): it was a brunette and winsome heiress turned career girl named Debbie Dean. After a promising start, the strip turned into a straight soap opera, and disappeared toward the end of the decade. © New York Post Syndicate.

Ellen Dolan, Will Eisner ("The Spirit"). Ellen Dolan was the somewhat neglected girlfriend of the masked justice-fighter known as The Spirit. Only the blonde ingenue and her father, the gruff Police Commissioner of Central City, knew that The Spirit was in reality Denny Colt, a criminologist believed dead by everybody else. In her double capacity as bearer of the flame and keeper of the secret, Ellen was oftentimes involved in lurking danger from which she was always rescued—in the nick of time, of course—by her boyfriend hero.

Lorelei Rox, Will Eisner ("The Spirit"). The greatest danger to Ellen, however, came from the many vamps that The Spirit encountered, most of whom took an immediate fancy to the masked hero. They were women with seductive manners, outstanding figures and evocative names. In addition to Lorelei—a modern siren luring unsuspecting mariners to their death—there were Autumn Mews, Sparrow Fallon, Wisp O'Smoke, Plaster of Paris, Silk Satin, P'Gell, and countless others. © Will Eisner.

Lady Jaguar, Frank Robbins ("Johnny Hazard"). Johnny Hazard, pilot and adventurer extraordinaire, was also to meet a variety of femmes fatales in the course of a prolific career started in 1944. One of the most memorable was undoubtedly the animal tamer known as Lady Jaguar, who used her ruthless talents to train wild tigers as well as keep two-legged wolves at bay. © King Features Syndicate.

Grandma, Charles Kuhn. Among comic strip women the young and sexy girls have traditionally occupied center stage. One exception to the rule was the feisty old curmudgeon known simply as Grandma, whose spirit proved as young as that of the children she was always befriending. (The strip made its debut in 1947.) © King Features Syndicate.

YEAH, I LIKE T' FISH AT NIGHT!

Blondie, Chic Young. In 1933 Blondie finally married Dagwood (who was thereupon promptly disinherited by his father). She then turned into a model wife: seen as the boss of the house and the holder of the purse strings, she also lavishes genuine affection on her bumbling husband and her two children, Alexander (seen here as a baby), and Cookie. "Blondie" is still as popular as ever in the hands of Chic Young's son, Dean, and James Raymond (Alex's brother).

THE FROLICSOME FIFTIES 1950-1959

From the beginning of their existence the American comics have exhibited a strong cyclical movement over the years, with one major theme or overriding trend giving way to a newer one. In the early years slapstick and humor dominated the scene, to such an extent that the newborn art form was promptly dubbed "the Comics," much to the chagrin of later commentators. In the 1920's it was the family that came to the fore; adventure was the major current among comic strips and comic books of the 1930's; and war was the dominant theme of the 1940's. In the decade of the 1950's, possibly under the influence of television, the soap-opera (a genre that has been defined as dealing with the most delicate problems in the most superficial way) came into its own in the comic pages. Publishers Syndicate (now Field Newspaper Syndicate) was primarily responsible for the trend, with their ushering-in, as far back as the 1930's, of a strip called **Apple Mary** (later changed to **Mary Worth**), about an old busybody who spent her time solving other people's problems. Reader response was only lukewarm at first, but the strip finally made it big in the latter half of the 1940's, unleashing a flood of "suds" over the comic pages.

The most skillful practitioner of the genre in the early 1950's was Dr. Nicholas Dallis, a psychiatrist turned comic strip writer who, in the space of a few years, had created **Rex Morgan, M.D.** and **Judge Parker.** These two irreproachable pillars of their respective professions had more than their share of female admirers. Judge Parker was finally to succumb and remarry (he had been a widower at the inception of the strip), but Rex Morgan still remains obdurately wedded to his job, in spite of the incessant hints dropped by his pretty assistant, nurse June Gale. As Richard Marschall, noted comics' historian, observed: "June Gale . . . is secretly in love with her boss; in return she receives appreciation and respect from Morgan." The stereotype of the salaried girl's unrequited love for her boss is, of course, a staple of soap-opera writing.

The tables were turned with Stan Drake's **The Heart of Juliet Jones**, whose two heroines, the somewhat priggish Juliet Jones, and her tempestuous younger sister, the aptly-named Eve, played tag with the heartstrings of the helpless males who fell in love with them. After a while Drake realized that Juliet (originally in her early 30's) was not growing any younger, and that her **femme fatale** role was becoming increasingly difficult to sustain, and he subsequently married her off, leaving the blonde-haired, kittenish Eve in charge of the whole field, a task she has been discharging with much gusto ever since.

Meantime the show-business syndrome, which had suffered a prolonged slump all through the 1930's and 40's, received a boost with the creation of Leonard Starr's **On Stage.** Its heroine was a naive, stage-struck, dark-haired young ingenue named Mary Perkins, who had come from the provinces to conquer Broadway. After a whirlwind debut Mary Perkins slowed down a bit, and now married, she displays the poise, assurance and aplomb that one would expect from a successful stage and movie actress. She is a mature, well-balanced, well-adjusted woman, not without similarity to Connie.

Leonard Starr has also been populating the **On Stage** strip with a variety of supporting or walk-on female characters, all depicted with much elegance of line, glamor and style. Whether they appear as Mary's rivals or her mixed-up friends, Starr's women constitute the most attractive feminine gallery since Alex Raymond's **Rip Kirby**.

In lively contrast to this seemingly too-proper lot, comics entrepreneur Jerry Iger (the man who deserves the most credit for the creation of **Sheena, Queen of the Jungle**) unleashed a fresh bevy of exotic beauties on an eager and appreciative public. Flamingo was a sexy Gypsy dancing girl, whose dark flowing hair and full-bodied figure held men in thrall, although she remained adamantly loyal to her American boyfriend, Joe. South Sea Girl was, as her appellation implied, a sarong-clad, orchid-bedecked Polynesian lovely, the dream-object of many a forlorn sailor. The adventures of both girls were rather conventional (though never dull) and were devised as a means of displaying their curvaceous figures to best advantage.

The fun provided by **Flamingo** and **South Sea Girl** was quite innocent. The 1950's also marked the high point of breast fetishism in the comics, and the trend's acknowledged master was Frank Frazetta who had been "ghosting" the **Li'l Abner** strip for the best part of the decade. Frazetta was the artist most responsible for Daisy Mae's over-generous bustline, and he consciously remodelled Moonbeam McSwine, the easy-on-the-eye, hard-on-the-nostrils swineherder's daughter, after Jane Russell's ample proportions. Before joining the Al Capp assembly line, Frazetta had practiced his mammary proclivities on a variety of comic book females (notably on the prehistoric, skimpily fur-clad Pha in **Thun'da**) and in his own short-lived sports strip, **Johnny Comet.**

Bob Lubbers, who teamed up with the aforementioned Capp to create **Long Sam**, belonged to the same school, but in a less blatant way, which may account for his lesser fame among **aficionados** of the genre. Long Sam was a leggy, bosomy and incredibly naive hillbilly girl who had never been allowed to see a man, at the time the action opened. She later made up for her ignorance in a variety of ways, but the leering undertones of the strip began to get tiresome after a while, and it was discontinued in the early 1960's.

In the 1950's comic book titles were sprouting female spin-offs in all directions. Bob Kane (perhaps spurred on by Dr. Fredric Wertham's dark intimations of homosexual hanky-panky going on between Batman and his young ward Robin) decided to add Batgirl and Batwoman to the dynamic duo of crime-fighters, as a sexual balance to the Caped Crusader and Boy Wonder. The effort was only half-hearted (and half-baked) and it never amounted to much.

Supergirl proved to be another matter. The "Girl of Steel" was, like Superman, a refugee from the doomed planet Krypton (in the original story Superman had been the lone survivor, but in later years editors and scriptwriters added more and more survivors, until there were enough of them to populate a medium-sized town). At any rate Supergirl turned out to be Superman's cousin and, in the best tradition of the genre, adopted the secret identity of Linda Lee Danvers. A blonde teenager when wearing her costume and a bewigged brown-haired high school student in mufti, Supergirl performed her amazing feats in the grim, self-righteous tradition of the Superman family. She also managed to keep romance out of her life in both her guises—she was, to put it succinctly, a super-square.

New comic features were being turned out at a fairly decent rate in the 1950's. If original female creations failed to keep pace with the new strips, it was due, in great part, to the decline of the story-strips (in which there is a greater opportunity to develop a variety of believable characters), and the multiplication of humor strips (**Beetle Bailey**, **Dennis the Menace**, **Peanuts**, etc.) practically devoid of sexual differentiation, an almost full circle back to the situation that prevailed in the early years of the comic medium.

Mary Worth, Ken Ernst and Allen Saunders. Mary Worth started her long career in the comics in 1932, when she was known as Apple Mary. She underwent a complete social metamorphosis in the 1940's, when the combined talents of writer Allen Saunders and artist Ken Ernst helped lift her out of the slightly tawdry existence she had led in the 1930's into a life of comfort and ease, where most of her time is spent in dispensing advice to the lovelorn and the (fashionably) distressed, like an unpaid Dear Abby. "Mary Worth" hit its stride in the 1950's, when it became the most successful of all soap-opera strips.

Mary Perkins, Leonard Starr. A bubbly brunette named Mary Perkins perked onto the New York stage in 1957, looking for fame and fortune on the Great White Way (as it was then known). In true soap-opera fashion, she finally found both (and a handsome and considerate husband to boot), not without a long string of disappointments and agonies, however. "Mary Perkins" (also known as "On Stage") is one of the most agreeably drawn of the current newspaper strips. © Chicago Tribune-New York News Syndicate.

Juliet Jones, Stan Drake. Juliet Jones began life (in her 30's) as a younger and more glamorous copy of Mary Worth. She was also more energetic, getting herself involved in as many predicaments as she helped others solve, even successfully running for the mayoralty of her home town. Her heart (the strip is officially known as "The Heart of Juliet Jones") had throbbed for many an eligible man before finally settling on criminal lawyer Owen Cantrell, whom Juliet married in 1970, after 17 stormy years of spinsterhood. © King Features Syndicate.

Eve Jones, Stan Drake ("The Heart of Juliet Jones"). Juliet Jones's younger sister, Eve had always displayed a more flamboyant lifestyle than her slightly priggish sibling. She has also become the central character of the strip following Juliet's marriage. © King Features Syndicate.

June Gale, Nicholas Dallis and Marvin Bradley ("Rex Morgan, M.D."). Not all comic strip soap-operas have female leads (though many do). When such a strip is carried by a male, custom has it to put an unmarried young woman (usually devoured with secret passion) by his side. Rex Morgan is a dedicated physician, and June Gale, his assistant, runs true to stereotype. Hard as it is to believe, Rex and June have carried on their platonic relationship since 1948. © Field Newspaper Syndicate.

Abbey Spencer, Nicholas Dallis and Harold LeDoux ("Judge Parker"). Unlike June, Abbey Spencer is not in love with the title character but is instead the lively girlfriend of attorney Sam Driver, another principal in the strip. The plotlines, however, are cut out of the same threadbare cloth by old hand Nick Dallis, who started the feature in 1952. © King Features Syndicate.

Long Sam, Bob Lubbers. Bob Lubbers's motto has always been **"cherchez la femme,"** and his talents in this genre have never been displayed to better advantage than in "Long Sam." Sam was a girl, and Lubbers's lush style of drawing left no one in doubt of the fact; her fulsome figure accorded to the canons of feminine beauty prevalent in the decade, and she disappeared in 1962, after an eight-year career. © United Feature Syndicate.

Peggy, Ken Bald ("Judd Saxon"). The helpful, intelligent—but not too intelligent—secretary with the legendary heart of gold (and a lovely figure to match), Peggy was not in love with the boss, but with Judd Saxon, a bright young executive on his way up the corporate ladder. Peggy was always ready with advice and help in the background. Judd, however, was only in love with his own aspirations and ambitions. A typical status-worshipping strip of the 1950's, "Judd Saxon" (which started in 1957) only survived till 1963. © King Features Syndicate.

Lucy Baker, José-Luis Salinas ("The Cisco Kid"). Lucy Baker was a strong-headed young lady with all the requisite qualities for survival on the Western frontier (where the strip was set). A blonde, self-reliant early fighter for women's rights, she did not succumb easily to the Cisco Kid's underhanded advances, nor to the threats of townspeople incensed by her unconventional ways and her suffragette views. © King Features Syndicate.

Mamie, Russell Patterson. Russell Patterson was one of the more inspired depicters of feminine beauty. His haughty, upper-class beauties had been dominating the magazine scene for a long time when he created "Mamie" in 1951. Mamie was a slightly more down-to-earth character than his earlier creations, but she was stylish to her fingernails and always sported the latest fashions. In spite—or because—of its elegance and glamor, the strip folded in 1956. © United Feature Syndicate.

Bobbie Burnem, Bill Overgard ("Steve Roper"). When "Big Chief Wahoo" started faltering in the 1940's, the author introduced a handsome blond adventurer named Steve Roper into the strip. It was only with the arrival of Bill Overgard (who took over the feature in 1953) that the strip acquired its slick, modern character. One of the attractions of the repolished version was Overgard's loving delineation of beautiful girls, such as the piquant, irresistible Bobbie Burnem. The strip (further altered to "Steve Roper and Mike Nomad") is still alive and well.

Moonbeam McSwine, Al Capp ("Li'l Abner"). Moonbeam McSwine was a gorgeous and natural beauty who tended pigs in all innocence. Visiting male characters would fall madly in love with her, until they got a whiff of her "perfume" . . . Frank Frazetta (who "ghosted" for Al Capp in the 1950's) gave Moonbeam her aggressive bustline, as well as the physical features for which she is best remembered.

Jean, Frank Frazetta ("Johnny Comet"). Prior to joining the Capp assembly line, Frazetta had been drawing the short-lived "Johnny Comet" (later retitled "Ace McCoy") in 1952–53. The strip was most notable for its well-endowed female characters, particularly Jean, girlfriend and stablemate of race-driver Johnny. © McNaught Syndicate.

Pha, Frank Frazetta ("Thun'da"). In the early 1950's Frazetta also drew "Thun'da," a comic book taking place in a lost world peopled with prehistoric monsters and cave dwellers. Pha, a luscious cave girl clad in a sarong-like fur outfit, was the hero's girlfriend and, by most accounts, the star of the show. © Sussex Publishing Co.

Flamingo, Matt Baker. Flamingo was a dark-haired, full-bodied Gypsy dancer whose adventures took her all over Europe. In her righteous endeavors she was assisted by the entire tribe of her fellow Gypsies and by her grandfather, Pepo, the mask-maker. She started her comic strip career in 1952, and ended it one year later with marriage to her only love, an American named Joe. © Phoenix Features.

South Sea Girl, Matt Baker. The heroine of this exotic adventure strip was a Polynesian beauty named Alane, straight out of Dorothy Lamour jungle films, right down to the sarong. Her involvements with shady operators, gun runners and diamond smugglers were made even more entertaining by her amazing displays of physical prowess. © Phoenix Features.

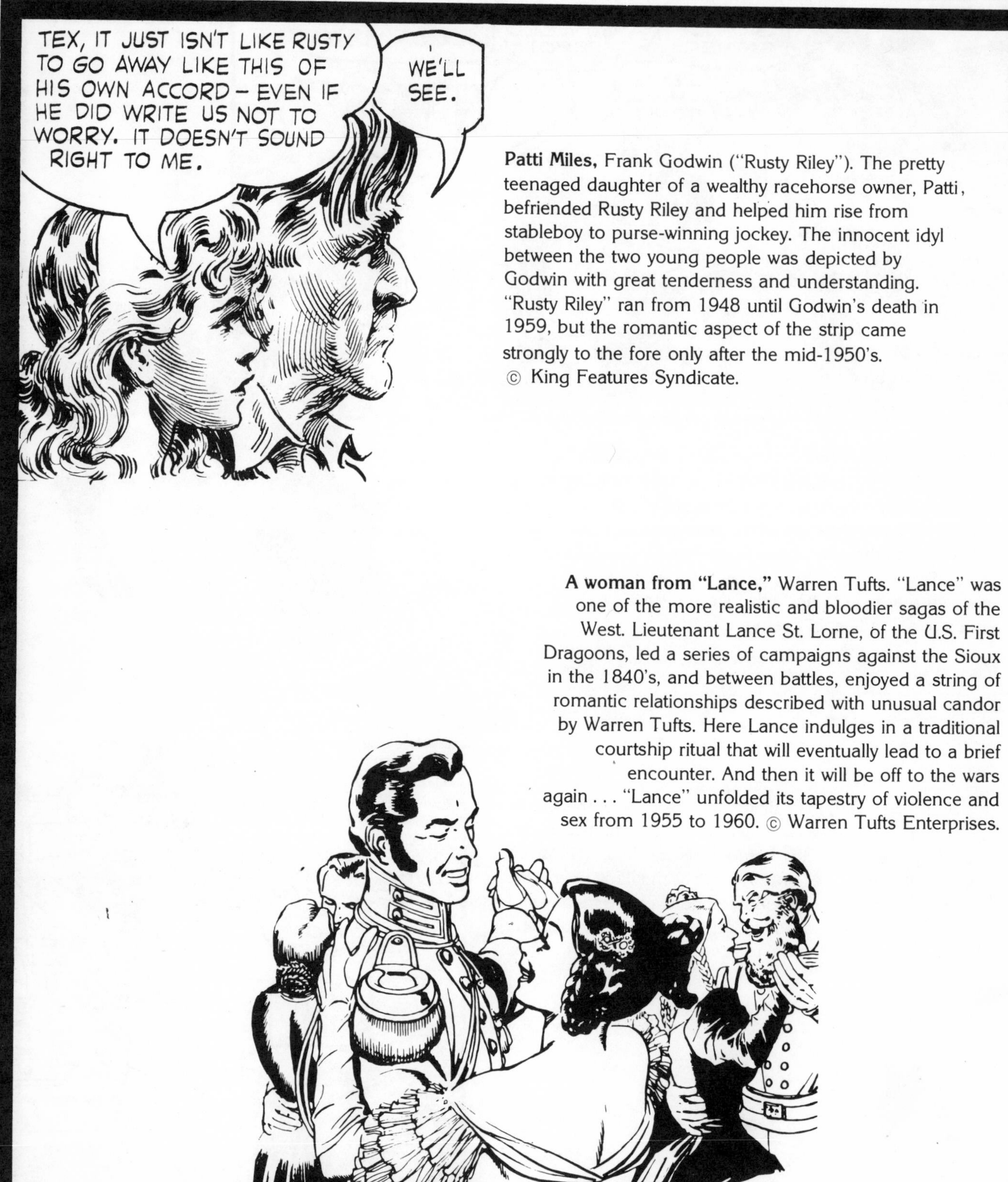

Patti Miles, Frank Godwin ("Rusty Riley"). The pretty teenaged daughter of a wealthy racehorse owner, Patti, befriended Rusty Riley and helped him rise from stableboy to purse-winning jockey. The innocent idyl between the two young people was depicted by Godwin with great tenderness and understanding. "Rusty Riley" ran from 1948 until Godwin's death in 1959, but the romantic aspect of the strip came strongly to the fore only after the mid-1950's.

A woman from "Lance," Warren Tufts. "Lance" was one of the more realistic and bloodier sagas of the West. Lieutenant Lance St. Lorne, of the U.S. First Dragoons, led a series of campaigns against the Sioux in the 1840's, and between battles, enjoyed a string of romantic relationships described with unusual candor by Warren Tufts. Here Lance indulges in a traditional courtship ritual that will eventually lead to a brief encounter. And then it will be off to the wars again . . . "Lance" unfolded its tapestry of violence and sex from 1955 to 1960.

Lucy Van Pelt, Charles Schulz ("Peanuts"). Lucy is without a doubt the best-known female character to come out of the comics world of the 1950's. As Charlie Brown's chief tormentor, and the scourge of the little band of preschoolers that populate the Peanuts cast, she already exhibits all the characteristics of ruthlessness and deceit that will make her into the successful person she dreams of becoming. Her only weakness is her unrequited love for the music-loving Schroeder, whom she pursues with her typical willfullness. "Peanuts" has been strong ever since its inception in 1950. © United Feature Syndicate.

Miss Peach, Mell Lazarus. Miss Peach is the angelic teacher and guardian angel of the most unruly bunch of young brats ever to disturb a classroom. While upstaged most of the time by her young charges, Miss Peach, snub nosed and daintily pretty, always manages to keep her sunshiny disposition, even in the face of the most outrageous provocations.
© Field Newspaper Syndicate.

Jane Calamity, Lina Buffolente. Lina Buffolente is one of the few women cartoonists active in the field of Italian comic strips. Her forte is the Western, and she has taken advantage of her position to strike an early blow for women's rights with her spirited depiction in the 1950's of that legendary heroine, "Jane Calamity," as Calamity Jane is commonly known in Italy. © Lina Buffolente.

Gay Abandon, Stan Lynde ("Rick O'Shay"). Gay was the one-time saloon singer and shady lady of the frontier town of Conniption. Reformed by the love of marshal Rick O'Shay (himself a reconstructed gambler), Gay is now leading the respectable life of housewife and mother, much to the chagrin of many readers who appreciated her better in her former role. "Rick O'Shay" has been appearing since 1958. © Chicago Tribune-New York News Syndicate.

Carol Day, David Wright. This gorgeous and lovely cover girl has known many adventures, not all of them romantic, since her first appearance in the London Daily Mail in 1956. At Wright's death in 1967 the "Carol Day" strip passed into the hands of Kenneth Inns. © Daily Mail.

Supergirl ("Superman"). Supergirl came into being in 1959, as a further addition to the Superman family. She was the daughter of scientist Zor-el (himself the brother of Superman's father Jor-el), and therefore Superman's cousin. Sent to earth by her father to escape her native planet Krypton's imminent disintegration, she became the female counterpart of the Man of Steel. (It is worth noting that Supergirl's origin is an exact rehash of the birth of Superman; it speaks volumes about the imagination and originality of the editors at DC Comics.) © DC Comics Inc.

Dilly, Mel Casson and Al Andriola. Dilly was one more among the bachelor girls who were a staple of 1950's strips. She was drawn with great gusto, but her adventures lacked punch. The strip (titled "It's Me, Dilly!") ran from 1958 to 1962. © Hall Syndicate.

MEET MY BOSSES...

THEY'RE SLAVE DRIVERS AND TYRANTS—AND THEY DECIDE **EVERYTHING** FOR ME...

HOW I EARN MY LIVING..

("LET'S MAKE HER A MODEL!")

WHERE I GO FOR LOCATION SHOTS..

("WHEREVER **WE** FEEL LIKE GOING!")

HOW I MAKE-UP MY LIPS..

("FULLER —MORE LUSCIOUS!")

WHAT COLOR MY HAIR SHOULD BE..

("A BLONDE - NATURALLY!")

WHAT CLOTHES I'LL WEAR..

("THAT'S A **RAG**— THAT'S FOR YOU!")

...EVEN THE BOYS I GO OUT WITH!...

BUT WHILE I'M OUT HAVING FUN, THEY'RE TRYING TO BEAT DEAD-LINES SO THAT ALL OF YOU CAN READ "IT'S ME, DILLY!"

Lois, Mort Walker and Dik Browne. Lois Flagston (the better half of "Hi and Lois") is perhaps the most warm, charming and winsome of all comic strip housewives. She runs the family with a light touch and a sure hand. Hi and Lois form a loving twosome, a far cry from the traditional bickering couples of the funnies. Their brood, made up of the mop-haired Chip, the mischievous twins Dot and Ditto, and Trixie, the thinking baby, are equally endearing. The whole family has been a favorite of comic readers since the inception of the strip in 1954. © King Features Syndicate.

The Batwoman, Bob Kane ("Batman"). Superhero families were all the craze in the 1950's, and Batman was soon saddled (starting in 1956) with a female associate, a former circus performer known as The Batwoman. © DC Comics Inc.

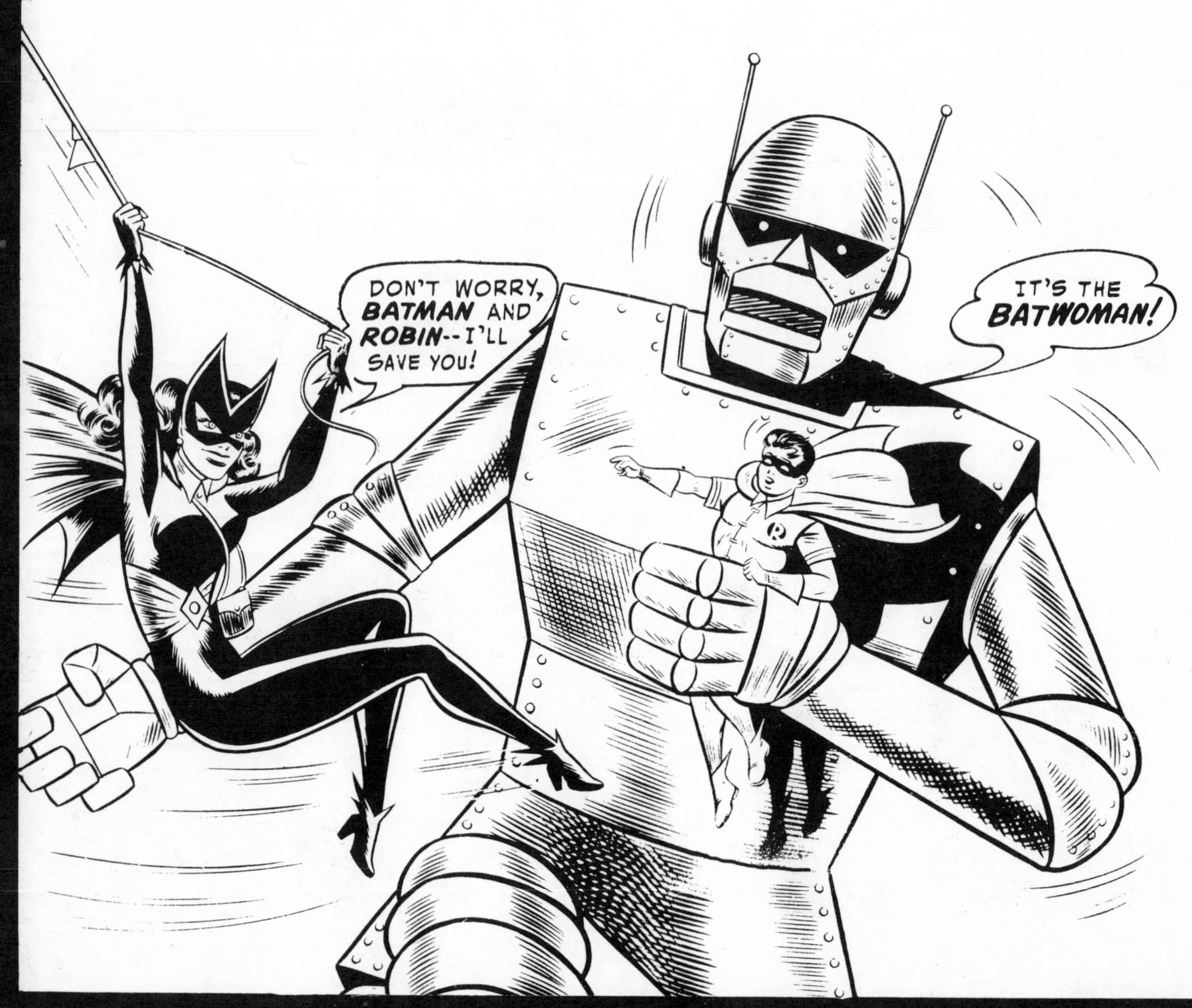

The Jackson Twins, Dick Brooks. This pair of identical-looking and engaging teenage girls have been playing innocent tricks on their friends and relations since the early 1950's. Jill is on the left, and Jean is on the right; or is it Jill on the right, and Jean on the left? © McNaught Syndicate.

Batgirl, Bob Kane ("Batman"). Pleased with the acceptance of The Batwoman among readers, DC editors soon came up (in 1961) with a teenage equivalent, Batgirl, Batman's niece. This preponderance of female relatives was supposed to generate readership among young women. © DC Comics Inc.

YOU'VE COME A LONG WAY, BABY 1960-1977

7

The last 17 years have been marked by a series of social upheavals, and especially by what has come to be called "the sexual revolution," yet it would be difficult—indeed almost impossible—to find a reflection of these far-reaching events in the newspaper strips of the last decade and a half. In contrast to earlier times when the comics had held up a mirror to the society around them, the syndicated strips were now 15 or 20 years behind the times in social outlook. This flight from reality has been responsible, above anything else, for the rapid shrinking of newspaper strip readership in the 1960's and 1970's, especially among younger people.

Instead of trying to update their comics in order to appeal to a more sophisticated audience, syndicate editors decided to hold on, at any cost, to the readership that was left. Newspaper strips were thus deliberately aimed at "the old lady in Dubuque," to the exclusion of anything that might smack of modernism, and this ostrich-like policy led to some grotesque situations. At a time when the institution of marriage had become irrelevant to a growing number of couples, cartoonists were ordered to rush off their protagonists into wedlock (accelerating a trend that had begun in the late 1940's): Steve Canyon has recently married, and so have Juliet Jones and Brenda Starr (to much accompanying publicity). Other, more relevant, problems have been swept under the rug to such an extent that, when Allen Saunders introduced an unwed mother into his **Mary Worth** strip, in 1976 (in 1976!), this event was deemed so revolutionary that the **New York Times** published a story about it.

In view of the foregoing it is therefore not surprising that only a handful of noteworthy female creations have come into being since 1960. In **Apartment 3-G** (now titled **The Girls of Apartment 3-G**) the prolific Dr. Dallis introduced three attractive career girls sharing the same New York apartment: the brunette Margo Magee, a secretary; the red-headed Tommy Thompson, a nurse; and the blonde school-teacher Lu Ann Powers. Their attractiveness owes more, however, to artist Alex Kotzky's suitably graceful penwork than to Dallis's often muddled plots. Bob Lubbers tried his hand at another girl strip, **Robin Malone**, which lasted only one year, and a novel approach was tried with **Friday Foster**, which for the first time presented a black girl as a comic strip heroine; it didn't last either. **Captain Kate** was a valiant try at reviving the 1930's tradition of adventure strip heroines (in this case the female skipper of a 18th century privateering ship sailing the Seven Seas). More recently Stan

Lee has come up with **The Virtue of Vera Valiant**, about a young woman unable to cope with all the ordeals that befall her, in the manner of the highly successful TV soap-opera spoof, **Mary Hartman, Mary Hartman.**

It took Garry Trudeau, who had already broken a number of other taboos in his iconoclastic **Doonesbury**, to bring some real-life contemporary female types back into the comic pages. The most popular are Virginia ("Ginny"), a liberated black law student and candidate for Congress, and her roommate, Joanie Caucus, who at age 40-plus walked out on her husband and children to enroll in law school.

Because they sell directly to the public (while syndicate editors only sell to newspaper editors, a very incestuous relationship), comic book editors have proved somewhat more imaginative: the 1960's were the age of relevance for comic book writers, and while this concern somewhat abated in the 1970's, it never quite died out. Interestingly enough it was during this period that two of the most morbidly fascinating female creations saw the light of print in comic book format. One was Vampirella, the black-tressed, succinctly-clad vampiress who had fled the dying planet Drakulon to replenish her blood supply here, on good planet Earth, where she was to meet and subdue a number of male opponents in her insatiable search for human blood; and the other the fiery-haired, fierce-tempered Red Sonja, a sword-wielding, man-baiting adventuress, clear out of the dark night of history, when only might made right, and no mercy was given. These were fighting, cursing she-wolves, not likely to knuckle under to any man.

Other interesting female creations came out of the comic book pages, notably Sue Richards ("Invisible Girl"), of **The Fantastic Four,** and the inexhaustible array of scheming, sex-crazy women whom Conan the Barbarian encounters in the course of his endless wanderings.

The 1960's saw the birth and flowering of the so-called underground comics which were bent on the destruction of every conceivable taboo of the medium. The movement's guru was Robert Crumb, and he created, in his stories, a number of memorable female characters, from the good-hearted, and sexually much put-upon black girl, Angelfood McSpade, to the stridently feminist Lenore Goldberg. Crumb's over-sized, over-sexed females drew fire from a number of feminist groups, and the artist was branded a male chauvinist pig. Another juicy underground creation of the same ilk (or, more accurately, of the same ink) was Denis Kitchen's Ingrid the Bitch, a precocious five-year old whose sexual cravings could only be satisfied by her libidinous canine companion, Pooch.

Because of these and other frolicsome creations, the undergrounders did run afoul of the law on a number of occasions, but they were ultimately vindicated. (One of their number, cartoonist Trina Robbins, made her contribution to the woman's liberation movement with several aggressively liberated women of her own imagining.)

While their rather egregious excesses might have put off the more traditional segment of the comics-reading public, the underground cartoonists unarguably brought a breath of fresh air into the stale sexual politics of 1960's comics and, on this score as on many others, they offered a number of models to later (and straighter) comic artists.

European cartoonists had, up to then, made only minor contributions to feminine iconography, mainly because European comics put stress on plot at the expense of character. This situation was drastically transformed with the appearance, in the early 1960's, of Jean-Claude Forest's **Barbarella.** This scantily-clad (when clad at all), sex-loving blonde astronaut (who bore more than passing resemblance to Brigitte Bardot) blazed a trail among European cartoonists even wider than the one she blazed among the planets. Soon a horde of cheap imitations sprang up over the continent, all of them uninhibited, unbridled creatures with such enticing names as Uranella, Messalina, Auranella, Angelica . . .

Of quite another mettle is the very British Modesty Blaise who came along around the same time. A former war refugee and boss of an international crime syndicate, Modesty later became an unpaid agent for English Intelligence. A master of judo and karate, and equally handy with gun and knife, she has been the nemesis of countless spies, mafia chiefs, and international outlaws. Her sex life, however, while active (by implication only) has been quite subdued in comparison with the more flamboyant exploits of Barbarella. (It should be noted that both **Barbarella** and **Modesty Blaise** were made into expensive movies with major directors, Roger Vadim for the former, Joseph Losey in the case of the latter.)

Once they were on their way apparently nothing could stop the British. In addition to **Tiffany Jones**, a soap-opera of undeniable qualities, as these things go, created by the all-woman team of Pat Tourret and Jenny Butterworth (also syndicated in the United States), they produced **Scarth**, the closest anyone has yet come to duplicating **Barbarella**'s appeal. As English comics historian Denis Gifford stated, Scarth "became the first full frontal nude female in British newspaper strips." Taking place in the future, the strip had the always near-naked Scarth scurrying around the galaxies, where she met the weirdest creatures, including a bearded hermaphrodite and a civilization of women-warriors.

The French took up the challenge in a typically Gallic way. Guy Pellaert brought out **Jodelle**, set in ancient Rome, with campy touches of New York and Las Vegas thrown in (such as neon signs inviting the populace to come see the Christians tossed to the lions, and toga-clad majorettes). It featured a sadistic and plotting Proconsuless, a lesbian masterspy, a faggish Emperor Augustus, and an assortment of other kinky characters, in whose midst the red-haired and luscious Jodelle had a field day of fun and frolic.

Georges Pichard is another master of erotic comic art. He teamed up with Jacques Lob to produce **Blanche Epiphanie**, an unbridled spoof of turn-of-the century melodramas, complete with a naive and pure orphan girl, a greedy and lecherous old banker, and a fantomatic and masked avenger (riding on a bicycle). Pichard topped **Blanche** with another opus, **Paulette**, in which a victimized young girl goes through all the kinky vicissitudes that writer George Wolinski's feverish imagination could devise.

Other countries also came up with original and attractive feminine creations, in particular Spain with Enric Sío's haunting Lavinia, and Japan where Koo Kojima holds sway over a bevy of almond-eyed enchantresses.

In the United States **Playboy** was first to feature the new brand of erotic comic strips, with **Little Annie Fanny**, a **Mad**-like sexual satire, with a buxom blonde innocent as its title character. In the course of each monthly installment Annie barely manages to save her virtue from the avid clutches of lecherous bankers, libidinous movie tycoons, and others of the same ilk. As in the **Little Orphan Annie** strip that it is lampooning, Annie Fanny has a mysterious protector, the all-powerful billionaire Sugardaddy Bigbucks.

Evergreen magazine went one better with an unfettered imitation of the European comic book sex romps titled **Phoebe Zeit-Geist**. The beauteous Phoebe, after being snatched from the middle of a white-tie reception in Antwerp, was to know a series of harrowing ordeals at the hands of unreconstructed Nazis, sadistic Chinese storm troopers, necrophilic monks, and other assorted perverts, deviants and weirdos, only to find herself back at the same party from which she had been abducted, with her virtue not quite as intact as that of Annie Fanny.

Bondage and bizarre comics have, for a long time, been a staple of American pornographic bookshops; Eric Stanton paid them a tongue-in-cheek, yet affectionate tribute with **Sweet Gwendoline**. Gwen, based on a character created by John Alexander Scott Coutts, is a shapely brunette whose innocence is severely tested in a succession of bondage and masochistic adventures. Although sex acts are never depicted (in quaint deference to the more stringent regulations that governed pornography in by-gone days), **Sweet Gwendoline** is still a far cry from the usual run of Sunday comics.

The acknowledged master of this new school of comic art is, without a doubt, the Italian Guido Crepax, called by some "the Raphael of the comics." While Crepax's contributions have been many, he is best noted for his remarkable portrait gallery of hauntingly beautiful women; his most celebrated creation is Valentina, a dark-haired Roman beauty, with a delicate, sensitive face, modelled after that of the silent movie actress Louise Brooks, and a slender, willowy figure. All of Crepax's women, however, share this Madonna quality, and they also bear slightly plaintive names—Marina, Bianca, Anita. Their fragility and vulnerability make the nightmarish world into which the artist delights in plunging them, a world of baroque and splendid decadence, reeking of sensuality, cruelty and evil, all the more terrifying and bestial.

In the Fall of 1975 Crepax topped himself with a comic art version of **The Story of O** which is, in terms of visual splendor and graphic expressiveness, the ultimate statement on the decline of the West. It also provides us with an ironic illustration of the long road the comics have traveled in their depiction of sex and women: from total inhibition to total exhibition, or around the world in 80 years.

Whether one likes the trend or not, and despite the reluctance of newspaper and syndicate editors, comics now aspire to the treatment of themes once the exclusive province of novels, plays, movies and television.

The girls of apartment 3-G, Nicholas Dallis and Alex Kotzky. The irrepressible Dr. Dallis came up with one more soap-opera in 1962, "Apartment 3-G," about three unmarried career women who share an apartment: they are Lu Ann Powers, a schoolteacher, Tommy Thompson, a nurse, and Margo Magee, a secretary. Lu Ann is the only one who married in the strip, but her husband has been reported as missing in action in Vietnam, so she is again unencumbered by matrimonial ties. The plotlines of the feature are predictable, but special praise should be given to the artist, Alex Kotzky, whose sophisticated style reflects a very appealing exuberance, freshness and **joie de vivre**. Here the girls strike a typical pose in the company of their neighbor and mentor, Professor Papagoras, a very Hemingway-like character.

Joanie Caucus, Garry Trudeau ("Doonesbury"). This fortyish dropout from marriage first appeared at Walden Puddle Commune, in the company of the titular hero, Michael J. Doonesbury, in 1970. She has since graduated from law school and gone on to bigger and better things ("Dare to be great, Ms. Caucus!"). Joanie Caucus's unconventional lifestyle has now become as much a bone of contention with newspaper editors as Trudeau's political opinions, and the middle-aged swinger has seen herself banned from the comic pages time and again. © G.B. Trudeau.

Robin Malone, Bob Lubbers. In 1968 Lubbers once again tried his hand at a newspaper strip: this was "Robin Malone" and it featured a very eligible widow and the many suitors constantly at her feet. Robin received a less enthusiastic welcome from the readers, however, and by 1970 she was gone. © NEA Service.

Friday Foster, Jim Lawrence and Jorge Longaron. Friday Foster, the first black newspaper strip heroine, appeared in 1970. After landing a job in New York as a fashion photographer, Friday would fly around the world on one glamorous assignment after another. Accent was put on her sentimental life, and racial problems were only lightly touched on. The triteness of the storyline finally did "Friday Foster" in, despite some remarkable artwork by Longaron: the strip was discontinued in 1974. © Chicago Tribune–New York News Syndicate.

Captain Kate, Jerry and Hale Skelly. This comic strip, created in 1967, could easily pass for a 1930's series in its unbridled quest for action and adventure. Captain Kate was the very alluring skipper of a ship engaged in bloody action in the time of buccaneers and pirates (Hale was the scriptwriter, and Jerry the artist). © King Features Syndicate.

Honi, Dik Browne ("Hägar the Horrible"). Honi is the very nubile 16-year old daughter of the title character. This early advocate of women's rights has only contempt for the chores usually reserved for girls in the strictly male-oriented Viking society in which she lives, and her most ardent desire is to follow her father in his plundering raids. © King Features Syndicate.

Vera Valiant, Stan Lee and Jack Springer. Superhero creator Stan Lee took time out from his comic book work to originate (in 1976) this spoof of soap-operas, in a manner not a little reminiscent of the "Mary Hartman, Mary Hartman" TV program. Poor Vera is subjected to a number of horrendous emotional and psychological ordeals in which her mettle is severely tested (the strip is aptly called "The Virtue of Vera Valiant"). © Los Angeles Times.

Wendy Raven, John Saunders and Al McWilliams ("Dateline: Danger!"). In 1968 the success of the "I Spy" TV series, with its "integrated" protagonists (one black, one white), gave rise to an equivalent double act in the comics: "Dateline: Danger!" which sported two heroes, both reporters with the Global News Co., the black Danny Raven and the white Troy (short for Theodore Randolph Oscar Young). Wendy Raven was Danny's younger sister, and she often occupied center stage, especially in the episodes featuring the black extremist Robin Jackson. "Dateline: Danger!" came to an untimely close in 1974. © Field Newspaper Syndicate.

Hildegard Hamhocker, T.K. Ryan ("Tumbleweeds"). Poor, homely Hildegard is the resident spinster of the frontier town of Grimy Gulch. Her favorite reading matter is "the husband hunter's manual," and her target is the slow-moving cowpoke Tumbleweeds; Hildegard's ardent pursuing and Tumbleweeds's artful dodging provide some of the funniest byplay in this hilarious Western parody, which started in 1965. © King Features Syndicate.

Gretchen, Ken Bald ("Dr. Kildare"). "Dr. Kildare" was the first of a slew of comic strips spawned by the fantastic success of doctor series on television (it started in 1962). Dr. Kildare, a perennial intern at Blair General Hospital under the supervision of gruff, old Dr. Gillespie, is married to his job. None of the beautiful women who have crossed his path (and Gretchen is a good example) has been able to sway the handsome physician away from his self-inflicted celibacy. © King Features Syndicate.

Nicki, Neal Adams ("Ben Casey"). "Ben Casey" was another TV-inspired hospital feature. Ben Casey was more muscular than Kildare, and was sometimes known to stray from the path of strict virtue. Nicki was his most steady girlfriend, as it went. Also started in 1962, "Ben Casey" only lasted till 1966. © NEA Service.

Broom Hilda, Russ Myers. In spite of her unappealing appearance and her greenish complexion, Broom Hilda is a rather winning character. A witch by profession, she wields her wand with determination, if not always with effectiveness. Her black magic often boomerangs on her, and her spells seldom work, but she can, when aroused to the required pitch, fly through the air or unleash thunder and lightning. Her most dogged efforts, however, are aimed at trapping a suitable mate, but these have remained fruitless so far.

Flo, Reg Smythe ("Andy Capp"). "Andy Capp" originated in 1957 in the pages of the English Daily Mirror, but the strip really took off in the 1960's, after it started syndication in the United States. Andy Capp is undoubtedly the uncrowned head of the ne'er-do-wells and the layabouts: he is garrulous, bibulous, obstreperous and libidinous; he is also a liar, a cheat, and a bully. His wife, Flo, is much put upon, abused and exploited, yet she displays no sign of leaving her husband or even standing up to him. This strip would seem to go against the grain of modern sensibilities, yet "Andy Capp" is enjoying an almost unparalleled world-wide popularity. © Daily Mirror Ltd.

Molly, Bob Weber ("Moose"). Molly is the long-suffering wife of the cantankerous, shiftless and bibulous Moose Miller. Over the years she has learned to roll with the punches and developed a sure technique of coping with her husband. "Moose" has been around since 1964. © King Features Syndicate.

Tawney, Gordon Bess ("Redeye"). Tawney is a dark, long-tressed Indian beauty, the daughter of Chief Redeye, and the pride of the clan. Her love for the klutzy Tanglefoot, the most hapless brave ever to disgrace a war party, has caused her father many a headache. "Redeye" has woven its merry tapestry of goofy happenings and weird situations since 1967. © King Features Syndicate.

Ms. Marvel, Jim Mooney and Joe Sinnott. Billed as "the world's newest super-heroine sensation" (she saw the light of print in 1976), Ms. Marvel is in reality Carol Danvers, editor of the magazine "Woman". In her editorial capacity she takes on her boss, sexist publisher J. Jonah Jameson. When she dons cape and mask to become Ms. Marvel (no relation to the equally superheroic Marvel family) she can hold her own with the best of the male superheroes. © Marvel Comics Group.

Isis, Mike Vosburg and Vince Coletta. Another newcomer to the ranks of super-heroines, the Mighty Isis originally came into being on the Saturday morning TV screen; she was transported to the comic book medium in 1976. The Egyptian goddess Isis comes to life again (so the origin story goes) in the person of a modern young woman, Andrea Thomas, who is granted superhuman abilities by the power of a mystic amulet. Isis utilizes her special powers to fight crazed scientists and resurrected Nazis hell-bent on destroying the world, a favorite pursuit of comic book villains. © Filmation Associates.

Little Annie Fanny, Harvey Kurtzman and Will Elder. What started as a grown-up parody of "Little Orphan Annie" (complete with a wide-eyed, if physically over-endowed, innocent and her ubiquitous guardian, Sugardaddy Bigbucks) has now turned into a sophisticated sexual and political satire. Ever since her birth in 1962, Annie Fanny (whom comic book historian Joe Brancatelli has aptly characterized as "a sexual Pollyanna") has maintained her virtue intact, despite the lecherous advances of press agents, film producers and business tycoons, and the devious schemes of rightwing politicos, urban terrorists and Ku Klux Klansmen. © Playboy Magazine.

Invisible Girl, Stan Lee and Jack Kirby ("The Fantastic Four"). Susan Richards (née Storm), alias Invisible Girl, was one of a quartet of quarreling and rambunctious superheroes who burst into the scene in 1961 as "The Fantastic Four." The leader of the group was Reed Richards (Mr. Fantastic) who later became Sue's husband, and the other two were Johnny Storm, Sue's flaming brother, and Ben Grimm. The Fantastic Four were the first superheroes with problems, and Invisible Girl had more than her share, what with identity doubts and a father fixation on Mr. Fantastic. Now that she has married the intellectual Richards, her problems have become those of any married woman bursting to get loose. © Marvel Comics Group.

Spider-Woman, Marv Wolfman and Ron Wilson. Like many other heroines, Spider-Woman started her career on the wrong side of the law (in her case as a minion of a spy organization known as Hydra) before putting her super-powers at the service of justice. She now enjoys her own comic book. © Marvel Comics Group.

Red Sonja, Frank Thorne. "Know also, O prince, that in those selfsame days that Conan the Cimmerian did stalk the Hyborian kingdoms, one of the few swords worthy to cross with his was that of Red Sonja, warrior-woman out of majestic Hyrkania. Forced to flee her homeland because she spurned the advances of a king and slew him instead, she rode west across the Turanian Steppes and into the shadowed mists of legendry." So stated Robert E. Howard's fictional Nemedian Chronicles. The fiery-haired, fierce-tempered Sonja rode out of Howard's novels and into the comic book pages in 1975, and she has become a favorite of readers of both sexes ever since. © Marvel Comics Group.

Bêlit, Val Mayerik ("Conan the Barbarian"). Again the Nemedian Chronicles: "Hither came Conan, the Cimmerian, black-haired, sullen-eyed, sword in hand, a thief, a reaver, a slayer, with gigantic melancholies and gigantic mirth, to tread the jeweled thrones of the Earth under his sandaled feet." Conan had preceded his rival, Red Sonja, in the comic books by a full five years, having been sprung on an unsuspecting public in 1970. Bêlit, the female captain of a pirate ship, was the barbarian's lover, and the only woman in whom he would confide. © Marvel Comics Group.

Gwen, Stan Lee and John Romita ("Spider-Man"). Among the many girlfriends Spider-Man has been through in his alter-ego guise as Peter Parker, the timid high-school (and later college) student , none was as appealing as the star-crossed Gwendolyn Stacy, whose death brought hundreds of irate letters to the Marvel offices. © Marvel Comics Group.

Ingrid the Bitch, Denis Kitchen. This irrepressible five-year-old nymphet started on her round of sexual adventures in 1970, consorting (and cavorting) with such sundry characters as Al Capone, Kissinger and Superman: she found all of them wanting. The only being able to sexually satisfy her was her no less libidinous canine companion, Pooch. © Denis Kitchen.

Blanche Epiphanie, Georges Pichard and Jacques Lob. A spoof of turn-of-the-century tearjerkers, this comic strip had an innocent and lovely orphan girl as its protagonist. The well-endowed Blanche is the object of unrelenting attentions on the part of the old and libidinous banker Adolphus; but every time that the dastardly Adolphus seems on the verge of subduing the imploring maiden, the mysterious and masked avenger, Defendar, barges in, in the nick of time. © Lob and Pichard.

Momma, Mell Lazarus. Mell Lazarus came up with this prototype of the "Jewish mother" in 1970. Mrs. Hobbs ("Momma") is the embodiment of the mother hen syndrome. While she is always bragging about her children's achievements (real or fancied) to friends and neighbors, she is also prone to berate these same children for their shortcomings (usually their lack of consideration for her feelings). Her eye is especially stern on her two unmarried children, the ne'er-do-well Francis and the flighty MaryLou, whom she ordinarily pelts with a barrage of motherly advice and chicken soup. © Field Newspaper Syndicate.

Batgirl (second version), Bob Kane ("Batman"). After the original Batgirl had fizzled out with the readers, the indomitable editors at DC Comics tried again in 1966. This time Batgirl was the librarian daughter of Gotham City police commissioner Gordon; after work Barbara Gordon would eschew her meek demeanor and bland appearance to don the costume of justice-fighter Batgirl and speed to the assistance of Batman—whether the Caped Crusader liked it or not. © DC Comics.

Marion McKay, Evert Geradts. The Beauty and the Beast theme seems to run deep among underground cartoonists. In this 1973 variant Dutch artist Geradts presents the sexual fantasy of a cute little elephant hopelessly in love with Marion McKay, the human leader of an all-animal band. © Evert Geradts.

Angelfood McSpade, Robert Crumb. Angelfood first appeared in Zap Comix no. 2, in 1967. An African Amazon with an unbridled appetite for sex, this child of nature brought the wrath of the women's liberation movement upon Crumb, who was accused of sexist proclivities in his depiction of Angelfood's subjection to every male she chanced to encounter.

Lenore Goldberg, Robert Crumb. The second most famous Crumb female character fared no better. While an ardent women's libber and radical in her speeches, Lenore was revealed as a typical middle-class house-mother at heart. © Robert Crumb.

Comanche, Greg and Hermann. Comanche is the young, pretty (but tough) owner of a Wyoming cattle ranch. Her obvious affection for her foreman, the strong and taciturn Red Dust, does not prevent her from asserting her authority over her often rebellious subordinate when she feels that the occasion demands it. Comanche is a strong believer in the policy of "an iron hand in a velvet glove." © Editions du Lombard.

Vampirella, José Gonzalez. This lovely woman-vampire came to earth from the faraway planet Drakulon in 1969. The scantily-clad Vampirella spends more time fighting evil than hunting for human blood (the purported reason for her earthward trip). The Freudian implications of a beautiful young woman using feminine wiles to get her required allowance of blood from unsuspecting males is presumably not lost on the readers. © Warren Publications.

Maryara, Richard Corben ("Rowlf"). "Rowlf" is probably Corben's best-known work. It first appeared in a fanzine in 1969, but has been reprinted in an underground publication in 1971. An eerie twist on the legend of Beauty and the Beast, it tells of the strange love between a fair maiden named Maryara and her canine companion, Rowlf. Living in an undefined country in an undefined age, Maryara is saved from the clutches of a barbarian horde of invaders by her dog, whereupon the two flee into the wilderness to escape their pursuers, and to live together. © Richard Corben.

Barbarella, Jean-Claude Forest. When she first appeared between book covers in France in 1964 (two years after her creation in a monthly magazine), censors banned her; when she was later transplanted to the United States, an enthusiastic Newsweek book reviewer described her thusly: "Cruising among the planets like a female James Bond, Barbarella vanquishes evil and rewards, in her own particular way, all the handsome men she meets in outer space. And whether she is tussling with Strikno the sadistic hunter or turning her ray gun on weird, gelatinous monsters, she just cannot seem to avoid losing parts or all of her skin-tight space suit." Barbarella has enjoyed worldwide success ever since, and has helped revolutionize in no small way the contents of adult comics. © J.C. Forest.

Jodelle, Guy Pellaert. Hard on the heels of Barbarella came Jodelle, another Gallic confection of the same ilk. The adventures of this red-headed undercover agent in the time of Emperor Augustus of Rome were drawn in a hard-edged, Pop Art style by Guy Pellaert in 1966. © Le Terrain Vague.

Scarth, Luis Roca. Scarth was a beautiful and permissive space heroine, on the model of Barbarella. Attired in bizarre and revealing outfits (when dressed at all), she romped through the galaxies from 1969 to 1972, when her journey was rudely interrupted by a blue-nosed newspaper editor. © The Sun.

Lai-Lah, Esteban Maroto ("Wolff"). Wolff is a Spanish blood brother of Conan the Barbarian. Like Conan he meets countless numbers of alluring women in his adventures, none of them more fascinating and deadly than Lai-Lah (whose name purportedly means "the untouchable one"), the sorcerer's daughter. © Buru Lan.

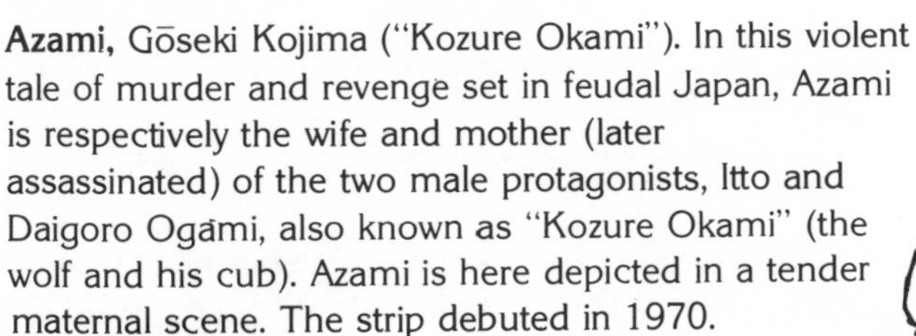

Azami, Gōseki Kojima ("Kozure Okami"). In this violent tale of murder and revenge set in feudal Japan, Azami is respectively the wife and mother (later assassinated) of the two male protagonists, Itto and Daigoro Ogămi, also known as "Kozure Okami" (the wolf and his cub). Azami is here depicted in a tender maternal scene. The strip debuted in 1970.

Stella Mix, William Brown and Mel Casson ("Mixed Singles"). Stella is a sharp-eyed operator who runs a singles-only apartment house, with the help of husband Harvey, in this light-hearted comedy of manners. "Mixed Singles" was created in 1972 by the writer/artist team of Mel Casson and William Brown (the latter is better-known for his authorship of the successful musical comedy, "The Wiz").

Tiffany Jones, Pat Tourret and Jenny Butterworth. Tiffany Jones was proudly introduced to the world by the all-woman team of artist Pat Tourret and writer Jenny Butterworth. Glowingly described by her creators as "the synthesis of all sixties girls, an all-systems-go girl," Tiffany has been weaving in and out of trouble in adventures that have taken her all over the world since 1964. © Associated Newspapers Ltd.

Françoise, Valentine and Chouka, Edouard Aidans and Michel Greg ("Les Panthères"). Françoise, Valentine and Chouka, collectively known as "the Panthers," are three young and pretty girls who had come from their province to conquer Paris and have made common cause against the world, after the fashion of the Three Musketeers. The strip, started in 1971, is not without similarity to "The Girls of Apartment 3-G," but its heroines are much more liberated. © Editions du Lombard.

Shary Flenniken, cover for **Wimmen's Comix. Wimmen's Comix** was started in the early 1970's as both a showcase for the talents of women cartoonists and a vehicle for the dissemination in comic strip form of the tenets and concerns of the women's movement. Among its more notable contributors have been Trina Robbins and Shary Flenniken. © Shary Flenniken.

Bibliography

The literature on the specific subject of women in the comics is small. This select bibliography includes books dealing with some general aspect of the subject within a larger (usually historical) framework, as well as books and articles directly devoted to the question. Monographs on a particular feature or character have been omitted.

I—Books

(On the general subject of comics only books in English are indicated; those volumes in a foreign language deal specifically—albeit from a narrow perspective—with women in the comics.)

Abel, Robert H., and David Manning White, eds. **The Funnies: An American Idiom.** New York: The Free Press of Glencoe, 1963.

Becker, Stephen. **Comic Art in America.** New York: Simon and Schuster, 1969.

Berger, Arthur Asa. **The Comic-Stripped American.** New York: Walker and Company, 1974.

Couperie, Pierre, and Horn, Maurice. **A History of the Comic Strip.** New York: Crown, 1968.

Daniel, Les. Comix: **A History of Comic Books in America.** New York: Outerbridge and Dienstfrey, 1971.

Estren, Mark. **A History of Underground Comics.** San Francisco: Straight Arrow Books, 1974.

Gasca, Luis. **Mujeres Fantásticas.** Barcelona: Editorial Lumen, 1969.

Horn, Maurice. **The World Encyclopedia of Comics.** New York: Chelsea House, 1976.

Lupoff, Richard, and Thompson, Donald, eds. **The Comic Book Book.** New Rochelle, New York: Arlington House, 1973.

Reitberger, Reinhold, and Fuchs, Wolfgang, **Comics: Anatomy of a Mass Medium.** Boston: Little, Brown, 1972.

Robinson, Jerry. **The Comics: An Illustrated History of Comic Strip Art.** New York: Putnam, 1974.

Sadoul, Jacques. **L'Enfer des Bulles.** Paris: J.-J. Pauvert, 1968.

Sadoul, Jacques. **Les Filles de Papier.** Paris: J.-J. Pauvert, 1971.

Sheridan, Martin. **Comics and Their Creators.** Boston: Hale, Cushman and Flint, 1942.

Steranko, James, ed. **The Steranko History of Comics.** Reading, Pennsylvania: Supergraphics (2 vols.), 1970 and 1972.

Waugh, Coulton. **The Comics.** New York: Macmillan, 1947.

Wertham, Fredric. **Seduction of the Innocent.** New York: Rinehart and Co., 1954.

II—Articles

(Only articles dealing in some significant way with the subject of women in the comics have been included.)

Amadieu, Georges. "L'Eternel Féminin Triomphe dans les Bandes Dessinées," in: **V-Magazine,** Winter 1968, Paris.

Barcus, Francis E. "The World of Sunday Comics," in: **The Funnies: An American Idiom.** New York, 1963.

Brüggeman, Theodor. "Das Bild der Frau in der Comics," in: **Studien zur Jugendliteratur,** 1956, Hamburg.

Buch, Hans-Christoph. "Sex-Revolte im Comic-Strip," in: **Pardon,** No. 12, 1966, Munich.

Chambon, Jacques. "Statut de la Femme dans les Bandes Dessinées d'Avant-Garde," in: **Mercury,** No 7, 1965, Paris.

Horn, Maurice. "Défense et Illustration de la Pin-Up dans la Bande Dessinée," in: **V-Magazine,** Fall 1965, Paris.

Macek, Carl. "Good Girl Art—An Introduction," in: **Comic Book Price Guide** (sixth edition). Cleveland, Tenn., 1976.

Mareuil, Chantal. "La Femme dans la Bande Dessinée," in: **Guida alla Mostra Internazionale dei Cartoonists,** Rapallo, Italy, 1976.

Mauriac, Claude. "De Modesty Blaise à Polly Maggoo," in: **Le Figaro Littéraire,** October 27, 1966, Paris.

Perini, Maria-Grazia. "Sexus Sequior," in: **Guida alla Mostra Internazionale dei Cartoonists,** Rapallo, Italy, 1976.

Saenger, Gerhart. "Male and Female Relations in the American Comic Strip," in: **Public Opinion Quarterly,** Summer 1949, Princeton, N.J. (reprinted in: **The Funnies: An American Idiom.** New York, 1963.

Walker, Mort. "Do Women Have a Sense of Humor?" in: **Guida alla Mostra Internazionale dei Cartoonists,** Rapallo, Italy, 1976.

A List of Women Cartoonists

Marjorie (Marge) Henderson, "Steaming Youth." © Marjorie Henderson.

This is a list of women cartoonists, and their created characters, who have made a marked contribution to comic strips and comic books. Foreign women cartoonists, as well as those American cartoonists who worked exclusively in the fields of editorial, magazine and newspaper cartoons, single-panel dailies or weeklies, and animation—and there are quite a few of them—are therefore not listed.

The cartoonists whose name is followed by an asterisk have been the subject of an entry in **The World Encyclopedia of Comics** (Chelsea House Publishers, 1976).

Mabel Burvik, under the pseudonym "Odin" (Dickie Dare)
Kate Carew (Handy Andy; The Angel Child)
Ruth Carroll (The Pussycat Princess)
Virginia Clark (Oh Diana!)
Dale Connor (Mary Worth's Family, as half of "Dale Allen")
Bertha Corbett (Sunbonnet Babies)
Fanny Cory* (Babe Bunting; Little Miss Muffet)
Grace Drayton* (Toodles: Dolly Dimples; The Pussycat Princess)
Edwina Dumm* under the pseudonym "Edwina" (The Meanderings of Minnie: Cap Stubbs and Tippie,
Shary Flenniken (Bonnie an' Trots)
Mary Gauerke (The Alumnae)
Alice Harvey (Sister Susie)
Ethel Hays (Flapper Fanny)
Marjorie Henderson under the pseudonym "Marge" (Little Lulu)
Virginia Huget (Campus Capers)
Selby Kelly (Pogo)
Marty Links (Bobby Sox; Emmy Lou)
Dale Messick* (Brenda Starr)
Tarpe Mills (The Cat-Man; Miss Fury)
Kate Murtah (Annie and Fanny)
Rose O'Neill* (The Kewpies)
Martha Orr (Apple Mary)
Kate Osann (Tizzy)
Gladys Parker (Flapper Fanny, Mopsy)
Trina Robbins (Vampirella)
Marie Severin (Doctor Strange; The Hulk; Sub-Mariner)
Hilda Terry (Teena)

Fanny Cory, "Little Miss Muffet." ©Fanny Y. Cory.

Edwina Dumm, "Tippie." ©George Matthew Adams Service.

Virginia Huget, "Campus Capers." ©Premier Syndicate.

Martha Orr, "Apple Mary." ©Publishers Syndicate.

Rose O'Neill, "The Kewpies." ©Rose O'Neill.

Trina Robbins, "Panthea." ©Trina Robbi

Index

F

G

H

I

J

K

L

T

U

V

W

Y

Z

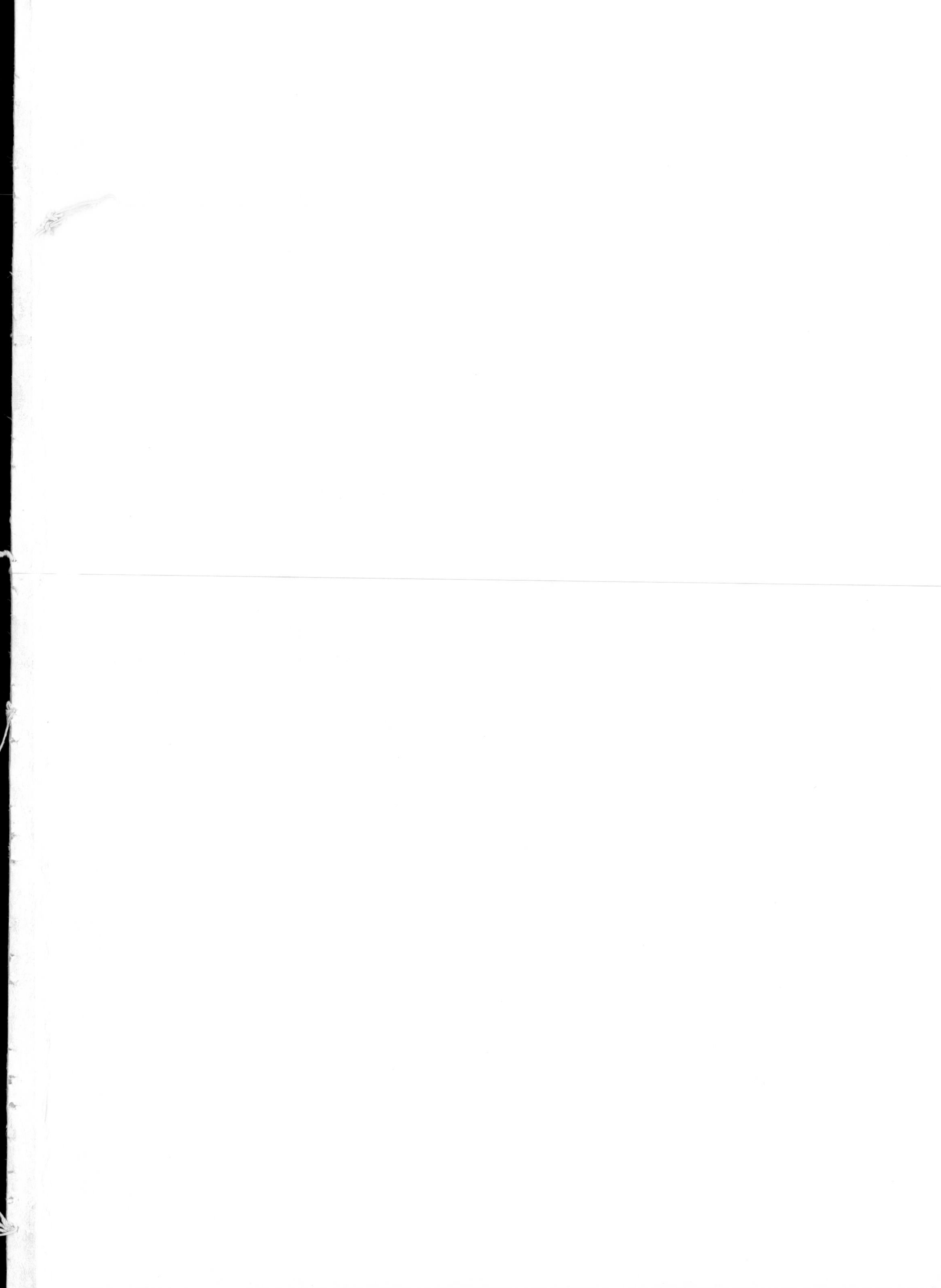